Turning Trials into Triumph

ROGER L WADE

ISBN 979-8-88751-221-1 (paperback)
ISBN 979-8-88751-222-8 (digital)

Christian Faith Publishing
832 Park Avenue
Meadville, PA 16335
www.christianfaithpublishing.com

Printed in the United States of America

Many people like me struggle daily with some sort of mental challenge. Relating to us can be difficult, but if people could learn about our challenges, we would be easier to understand and support.

I wrote this book for two reasons—to bring knowledge to those supporting us with ADD and to help those living with these challenges, needed support and encouragement. I will try to accomplish both.

I realized educating myself, believing in myself, and prayer made all the difference in the world—especially prayer.

If you tell God what you want—what you truly want— are willing to do the work and have patience and faith, what you desire will eventually come to you. Never give up!

To Kelli;

God Bless You

Roger L. Wade

Roger J Wade

In remembrance of my three lifelong friends: Billy Martin (1950–2022); Mike Morrison (Marion Michael Morrison, named after his uncle, John Wayne, 1953–2019); Don Rexon (1950–2012); and all the friends and family members we have lost in the past three years. May you all rest in peace, our new angels in heaven watching over us.

Contents

Introduction

Martha, Me, Joyce, and Mom when I was a year old

Until recent years, we didn't know much about attention deficit disorder. A lot of people could have had a better life knowing their problems weren't really with themselves. But I guess that's all part of growing. I hope this book helps everyone learn more about ADD. I hope this book gives hope and encouragement to those with ADD. I had a hard time growing up, but I made it—and this is how it happened.

I was a small boy with a big dream of growing up to be a great singer like Elvis Presley. It all began one night when I was six years old. My mother had taken me to see the movie *Love Me Tender*. I knew in that moment I wanted to be a singer when I grew up. While watching the movie, I started crying. I so wanted to be like that man on the big screen. My stomach felt like it was on fire, and my heart felt as if it was going to break. Once I went so far as having my sister dye my hair jet-black so I could look like Elvis, but it didn't work.

I've always wanted to make people happy. I've always made everyone around me laugh when they were feeling down. I've had a lot of time to think about my past—the good, the bad, and the ugly. Like most people, if I could go back in time, I would have made a lot of changes. If you feel like you aren't getting anywhere in your life and want to quit, stop, and take a good look at where you have been, and the things you have done.

I feel God has a greater purpose for each of us in this life. No matter how hard things get, and although we might not have the answers right now, somewhere down the road all will become clear to us as our lives unfold.

As you read this book, you will see the trials I've been through, and the tests God has given me. When you feel as if life is fighting you every step of the way, you must fight back even harder. Every time you get knocked down, get up again. Every time you get pushed up against a wall, turn around and knock that wall down. You can't let anything stop you from achieving your dreams because it is your life to live the way you see fit. Just remember, what you want you must work for because it won't be given to you.

Don't let fear stand in the way of your progress. I have fought hard my entire life to become who I am today. I've lost much along the way, and at times, I even felt I'd lost my own sanity. But the best thing is, through it all, I never gave up—I never gave in. You'll see how my life changed as you read each chapter. I thank the Lord for the talent, healing, and blessings given me and granting me my wishes.

My first guitar

Chapter 1

My Early Years

I was born on July 14, 1950, in Kern General Hospital, Bakersfield, California. Because I was born with curvature of the spine, most of my younger years were spent on the chiropractor's table, attempting to help me walk properly. One hip was lower than the other, making it hard for me to walk. It's something I overcame with time. Another challenge I discovered in 2009 was being diagnosed with a severe case of attention deficit disorder. It is one of the reasons I am writing this book. If I can help one person faced with overwhelming challenges see the difficulties I faced and overcame in my life while having ADD, I'll know I have achieved my purpose.

I have two older sisters, Joyce and Martha, and an older brother Michael. Martha was the tomboy while Joyce was the prissy one. Mike was not around the family much. In his early years, he lived with our grandpa, and when he grew up, he joined the army. After his time in the service, he began working as a police officer in Ridgecrest, where we lived. I guess you could say Mike was the only career man in the family until I was older and started playing music. I have been playing music over sixty years—that is a long time! Everyone in our family is still living and doing well, thank the good Lord.

Growing up was very difficult for me. I always had a hard time concentrating, and at school, things were even worse. Most people haven't the slightest idea how hard it was, just living day to day, feeling so different from all the other kids. It took me longer to learn basic things, like reading, writing, spelling, and arithmetic. When I tried to read a book, I would read the same lines over and over, not knowing what I had read. I couldn't comprehend what was being said in class.

At school, I'd get in trouble because my teachers thought I was not paying attention. It was hard for me to sit still for long periods of time. My mind would start to wander as if I had no control over it. I'd stare off into the distance, not thinking of anything, just looking blank. I'd get so frustrated that I felt I was on fire inside. I got mad and sat there looking around the room until the teacher came by, smacking my desk to get my attention. Most of the time, I was made to stay inside while the other kids went out to play. I always felt I was being punished for something I didn't do. The other kids in class made fun of me, calling me names like "stupid" and "retard" because I had to stay in the classroom. I felt like the class dummy. It wouldn't be until I was in high school that one of my teachers tried to help me by sitting and working with me one on one.

There were days I would go home after school and sit on the edge of my bed in my room, trying to under-stand what was happening to me. I was falling into a deep depression. Why was I being punished for things I couldn't understand or had no control over? Why didn't anyone know what my problem was? Why didn't anyone try to help me? Why did I feel so alone most of the time? My mother tried to help me as much as she possibly could. When she came home after work, she would sit me down in front of her and read to me out of the encyclopedia, showing me pictures to help me understand what things meant. After a while, you could say I started understanding things by looking at pictures. My father and sisters didn't help—telling me how stupid I was. I thought that was all part of growing up.

Having a learning disability doesn't mean you are stupid, or you can't learn to do the things everyone else can do. I'm not a writer, but I'm writing this book, and I haven't the slightest idea how to write a book. Yet here it is— my life story. Spelling is not one of my strengths, so I am thankful for the spell check program on my computer.

I've been able to read two books in my entire life, so imagine how hard it is for me to write a book! But if I can accomplish my goals, so can you! All you need is determination and a vision.

I know there are those in this world who have a difficult time coping with life and have no idea which way to turn. Watch for the signs. Pay close attention to what your loved ones are doing and how they act. Having a hard time reading doesn't always mean you need glasses. Just take a little more time and help them. Be patient. Be understanding. I can't stress enough how important this is!

I would love to travel and help people like me. It's sad that most people have a difficult time understanding what attention deficit disorder is. Life as a kid would have been so much easier for me, and for millions of others like me, if people understood what ADD was all about. All I ever wanted was to be like everyone else—to be able to think, to understand, and to feel normal. Normal is getting up in the morning and going to school or work without that burning feeling of dread in the pit of my stomach. Normal is not having to face humility every time you step outside your door because you don't understand the meaning of life and how things are supposed to work. Deep frustration occurs when you try to read something, and then read it over and over—only to find you still have the same problem each time you try to read, each day—you can't make sense of anything.

Chapter 2

Home Sweet Home

Joyce, Roger, and Martha

My first home was in an officer's tent behind my grand-pa's house on his farm in Pond, California. We lived there for six months. I don't remember much about it—I was too young. Sometimes the smell the fresh grown alfalfa that grew around his place takes me back to that time. We eventually moved to Sunnymead, California. When I was two years old, my mother put me in my playpen while she was doing her housework. I guess she didn't realize my playpen was right next to her dresser where I could reach her lipstick. I grabbed it and did some fancy artwork on myself, my playpen, and the surrounding walls. Mom wasn't too happy when she walked into the room. I can still hear the song playing on the radio at the time—"This Old House."

We moved again to a house behind the railroad tracks in Hemet, California. My sisters would take me outside to play in our front yard, which wasn't far from the tracks. We didn't have a fence around the house, so I guess you could say we didn't really have a yard. Martha would tell me hobos were going to carry me off and eat me if I didn't stay away from the tracks. She was always trying to scare me. And you know what? It worked! I never went near those tracks!

Chapter 3

The Hog Ranch

Dad and me at Grand-Pa's place

Our new home was another army tent on a hog ranch up in the mountains outside of Hemet. This one had a wooden floor with a gas stove in the middle of it. I remember one day, Mom and Dad went up the dirt road to see my aunt and uncle, just a couple of houses away. They were only gone about thirty minutes. My sister Martha turned on the gas oven and then went to find a match. Plug your ears! That's right—she opened the door and lit the match. Kaboom! She was lucky. All she got was singed hair and eyebrows and didn't blow us to kingdom come.

The place where we lived had Brahman bulls wandering loose around the property, and they'd come right up to the front of the tent. Every time I went out to play, they were there.

One day, I took my brother's BB gun outside to play with it, which I wasn't supposed to do. I had no idea how to use it. I put the barrel on the ground and proceeded to pull the lever down to cock it. I got it cocked, and with the lever still open, I just had to pull the trigger. I pulled the trigger, and it slammed back on my thumb. The bad thing was that it cut my thumb and hurt like the dickens. The good thing was I never sucked my thumb again. Now I have a nice long scar on my thumb that will always remind me to shut the lever before pulling the trigger.

Some days, my dad would take me with him when he fed the hogs. There were hundreds of them! We would drive down the road, putting slop in the troughs. The smell was awful!

Every morning, my mother would drive my brother and sisters down the mountain to their school, and almost daily, she would run over a rattlesnake or two.

We moved again; this time to a chicken ranch near Hemet. There were all kinds of animals—chicken, turkeys, cows, and skunks. Mom worked in the incubator room, checking the eggs before they went to market. She separated the bad ones from the good ones. Then she'd take the eggs with the chicks in them and put them in the hatchery for hatching.

One day, while Mom was at work, a skunk came running in. It didn't take Mom long to get out of there!

I had fun opening the door where the chickens were. As soon as I stepped inside, I'd slam the door and watch the chickens pull their heads back in their cages. I'd wait until they stuck their heads out again, and I'd clap my hands. I thought that was the funniest thing I'd ever seen. Now I realize how cruel it was and how it upset them.

When Mom said she was going out to kill a chicken for dinner, we'd all go out and watch her cut off the chicken's head. Then she'd let it go and it would run around in a circle until it dropped dead. Yep, my mother the chicken killer. Back then, that's how we survived.

A little boy named Kevin, who was my age, and I played together. His parents owned the ranch. Kevin and I would climb the hill behind our house and run up to a big pile of rocks. In the middle of the rocks was a big hole with water in it, full of crawdads. We'd take some string and bologna and try to catch them. When we got back home, we got in trouble. Mom said, "One of these days you're going to fall in that hole, and no one will ever find you!" We stayed away from the hole after that.

Some days, we'd go out and try to ride the calves in the pen, with not much success. Once every two or three months, the ranch hands would hang a cow up by its hind legs and butcher it right there in the field. The smell was so bad it made me sick to my stomach.

Next, we moved to McFarland, California. This was a short stay. I think we lived there four months, but during that time, a lot of things happened. The six of us lived in a very small apartment—just a living room with a hide-a-bed, one bathroom, and small kitchen area.

One day, we went to a park that was down the street from our apartment. My sisters were chasing me around the park. As I looked back to see how close they were, I turned around just in time to kiss the end of a picnic table. Lights out! The next thing I knew, I was in the hospital. That really messed up my mouth for a while. If that wasn't bad enough, a month later when I was climbing tree, I slipped and fell out of the tree. The worst part was hitting my mouth on a limb on the way down. Back to the hospital! Oh, I'm not finished yet—I saved the best for last!

All of us kids were playing hide-and-seek one night. As I ran around the corner of a house, another kid was running toward me with a stick in his hand. It went right through my arm at the elbow bend, right below my muscle. Where did I go? You're right—back to the hospital!

It was time for us to move again. I think it was time for me to stay out of the hospital!

On the chicken ranch; I'm the one with the hat.

I loved Davy Crocket.

Chapter 4

Trouble with the Law

The first time I was in trouble with the law was when we lived in a mobile home park in Oxnard, California, not far from the beach. A friend and I were playing jet pilots in the back of my dad's pickup truck. We were dropping dirt clod "bombs" on toy army men on the ground, watching them explode. We soon became bored. My friend told me about some glass bulbs he found in one of the yards in the park. We went exploring and found a big box of TV tubes in someone's yard. We didn't know any better, so we took the box over to the pickup. This was cool because when they hit the ground, they really exploded and popped. We were having a blast until we ran out of tubes. It was getting late, so we went home for dinner.

When I got home, Mom was cooking dinner and the smell made me hungry. We all settled in for some TV. Just as we were getting into the program, there came a knock on our front door. Mom opened the door to find two police officers standing there. Something in my gut told me I was in big trouble because my senses told me breaking those tubes wasn't right. Well, my mom had to pay for the tubes I broke, and then she proceeded to take it out on my butt.

All the kids in the park would go over and play in an old house that was deteriorating. I can still remember the musty smell and the beehive in one of the walls. My mother told us to stay away from the house because it was liable to fall in on us. But like most kids, we didn't always listen to our parents.

I woke up one bright, sunny morning and thought this would be a great day to play in the old house again. This time, when we walked through the front door there was a man hanging by a rope from one of the rafters. We ran screaming from the house, scared half out of our wits. We ran home to tell my mother what we had seen. My brother was standing in the living room laughing his head off. He and a few of his friends had made a dummy out of some old clothes they'd found and hung him from the rafter in the house to teach us a lesson. Lesson learned! We never played there again after that day.

Martha, Joyce, and me

Chapter 5

Friends Forever

We didn't live very far from the beach. I loved living there because I could smell the ocean every morning when I was getting ready for school. One day after school, I noticed a man watching all the kids as we got off the bus. He had Down's Syndrome, though I didn't know what that was at the time. I think he was in his early twenties. He was short but heavy. As the kids walked by, they laughed and made fun of him.

One afternoon when I got off the bus, I walked over, took his hand, told him my name, and we walked home together. We became the best of friends. After that day, every time I came home, he was waiting for me at the bus stop so he could walk me home. He was like a big brother to me. I guess you could say I loved him as much as my own brother. We did everything together. He had all kinds of toys we played with. He would put me up on his shoulders and give me a ride all over the mobile home park. He had a pet skunk named Stinky. We never took the skunk out of the cage, but we would stand there and watch him for hours.

My life seemed so perfect until that day when I got off the bus, and he wasn't there to meet me. I looked all over for Tommy, but he was nowhere to be found. When I got home, my mother told me to go to his house and see if he was home. Why didn't I think of that? I went to his house and found him playing with his trucks on the front porch. I walked up to him and asked, "Are you okay?" Just then his mother came out and said, "Go home and stay away from him. He isn't allowed to play with you anymore!" I stood there for a minute trying to figure out what I had done. I put my arms around his neck and started to cry. It broke my heart; he was the only friend I had. It was the worst day of my life. I cried all the way home. When my mom asked what happened, I told her what his mother told me. My mother walked over to me, put her arms around me, and said, "Don't cry. Things will be okay."

To this day, I still have a hard time talking to people about Tommy without becoming emotional. I think about him every time I see someone with Down's Syndrome. Later, Mom found out the reason I was not allowed to play with Tommy. His parents were afraid he might accidentally hurt me. I think I ended up being hurt more deeply being separated from Tommy than he could have ever done to me accidentally.

A short time after that, I was playing down the street from my house when three older boys, about four or five years older than I was, asked me if I wanted to see the fort they had built. I thought I had found some new friends to play with. When I went inside the fort, one of the boys pushed me down on the ground and the other two boys held me down while they took my pants off. One held my legs, and the other one held my arms while biggest boy climbed on top of me. When I started crying, the biggest of the boys put his hand over my mouth and told me if I didn't shut up, they were going to kill me and my family. In other words, I was being raped, and I couldn't do anything about it. I remember screaming for my mother, and my mind was going in circles. I was scared and all alone and didn't know what to do. As they walked away, I could hear them laughing. I heard one of the boys say they should go back and beat me up so I couldn't tell anyone. I got up and put my pants back on. I wanted to run away, but I was so afraid. I didn't know where to go. I sat there on the ground and cried for a long time before I finally got up and went home.

I walked in the house, but no one was home. I panicked. I went down the street and found my mother at her friend's house. My mom asked me, "What's wrong?"

I told her, "Everyone left me."

She said, "I'm still here and your sisters are with their friend's. Why are you crying?"

I thought about what the boys had said they would do to my mother, and I told her I was just scared. She took me by the hand, and we went home. I went into my room, crawled under my bed, and started crying into my pillow so she couldn't hear me. Then I drifted off to sleep.

Mom came in looking for me. Not seeing me on my bed, she looked under it, as she'd found me there many times before. She woke me up and said, "It's time for dinner." I was very quiet at the table, but then I was always a quiet little boy. I kept to myself most of the time after that. That was the first time in my life I remember feeling that I didn't belong in this world.

You can't imagine what it was like not being able to tell anyone about that day.

As the years went by, things seemed a little easier, even though I never forgot what those boys did to me that day. Even discussing it now is not easy, but at least I have healed enough to be able to speak about it openly without crying and deeply hurting inside. That is a blessing.

Not long after that frightening incident, we moved again—this time to Casitas Springs, California, near Ventura. I honestly looked forward to moving each time. It was exciting to me—new places, new adventures. I suppose all the moving around we did when I was growing up is where I get my periodic "urge" to move. I don't like to live in one place too long. However, this time I was more relieved to get away from those boys rather than excited to go somewhere new to live. I couldn't wait to get out of there and away from them forever.

Me in the trailer park in Oxnard, California

Chapter 6

Shot with an Arrow

I was ten years old when I really outdid myself. We lived in Casitas Springs in another mobile home park. This one was right at the base of a big mountain where Johnny Cash had built a house. I was always going up there to visit with his kids. My mother told us how dangerous it was climbing that mountain because of the lose shale. A new friend and I decided to climb it anyway. My friend wasn't too far behind me when I kicked a rock loose and it hit him in the head. We made it back to his house to get him fixed up. His sister was the only person home at the time, so she took care of his head. It was just a scratch.

A few days later, we were playing cowboys and Indians outside the trailer where I lived. My friend had a bow and a set of arrows. I was running across the street when he yelled at me. I stopped and turned around, just as he shot the arrow. It flew right toward me. I grabbed the arrow as it hit me and with a thud, I hit the ground. I stuck the arrow in my belt hole, so it looked like I had been shot—holding the arrow and making it appear to be sticking out of my belly. Play acting, I stumbled and fell in the dirt on my back. Our trailer was right next to where I fell, and my mother was at the kitchen sink washing dishes.

She looked up just about the time I hit the ground. I heard the door slam as she came running out of the house. She cleared the three-foot fence that surrounded our house without a problem. When she reached me, I sat up and started laughing, holding the arrow in my hand. I didn't laugh for long! As I recall, I was unable to sit down for a long time after that. That's a day I'll remember forever!

During our stay in Casita Springs, we became friends with Mr. and Mrs. Hooker who lived across the street. They took me deep-sea fishing with them on weekends. Their cocker spaniel rode in the back with me. We'd get on their boat, and out we'd go. I caught some of the biggest halibut on those trips, and we had so much fun. They taught me how to water ski, and I never once thought about what was beneath my skis. I'm glad I didn't see *Jaws* until later in life, or I'd never have gone out in the ocean!

This is the fence Mom cleared to get to me.

Chapter 7

Broken-Hearted

We moved again; this time to Bounds Road. It was a short street with maybe ten houses on it. At the end of the street was a lemon orchard. Our next-door neighbors were the Smiths: Fred; his wife, Gayle; and their three children—Freddy Jr., who was a year older than my older sister Joyce; Penny, who was the same age as my middle sister Martha; and Peggy, who was a little younger than me. Fred Sr. bought a Palomino horse, and they built a corral in the backyard for it. Peggy and I would go for rides through the lemon orchard all the time. It was a blast.

Across the street from our house lived the most beautiful girl in the world. Her name was Colleen. We were close friends. My mother would take us to the theater and drop us off while she did her weekly shopping. This was the first time I ever held a girl's hand. After a while her father decided he didn't want her to see me anymore. The next time I went to her house, she came out to tell me she had to stay away from me—we couldn't even be friends. Once again, I thought my life had ended.

My bedroom on Bounds Road

Chapter 8

Living like Gypsies

It seems we never lived in one place for over six months. Just when I began making friends, we would move again. It seemed like I was getting into trouble daily, but this time things went from bad to worse.

Both of my parents worked, so my mother made my sisters stay home and take care of me. That didn't make one of my sisters very happy. As soon as my parents left, all hell broke loose. My parents didn't even get out of the driveway before my sister began to take out her frustration on me. She would make me sit in a chair in the corner of the living room. If I got up, she'd push me back down in the chair and tell me not to get up again. I had to sit in that chair until my parents came home. If I told my mom what happened, my sister simply said she made me sit in the chair because I wouldn't mind.

The next day, it happened all over again, but worse than the day before. She must have figured out if she got away with it once, she had no worries. Next came the hitting and slapping if I got out of the chair. She told my other sister if she opened her mouth, she would get some of the same. I spent the whole day every day crying. My sister wouldn't even let me watch TV, and I had no clue why. One day, I'd had enough. When she pushed me down, I came up swinging. That was the day it stopped, and I was happy about that!

When my mother was at home, I went outside and played. We had a big fenced-in field next to our house where we could have horses. My father bought a horse, sight unseen. When the horse arrived at our home, we saw that it was beautiful, but high-spirited. My sister tried to ride it and the horse ran away with her. She never tried again. None of us got to ride him—not even my dad. The horse had to go.

I learned how to skate, and we began skating down the road next to our house. I got pretty good at dancing on skates. A brother and sister my age lived across the street from us. One day, we decided to take our skates and nail them to a two by four and ride it down the street. We called it a skateboard. This was around 1960. It wasn't until many years later skateboards were manufactured. We were the first!

My uncle brought over a Redbone Bloodhound for us to take care of. I loved that dog. I took Red for walks every day; actually, he took me for walks.

Before Red came into my life, I'd walk by a certain house where a big collie lived, and it would run toward me, snarling and growling. It scared me so much that I avoided that house on my walks. After I started walking Red, that scary dog never came out again. I thought Red was my savior, and I didn't have to worry about anything with him by my side.

On weekends, my mother would drop off my sisters and me to the swimming pool. We played in the shallow end of the pool because none of us could swim. I got out of the pool for a minute, and when I came back two older boys were splashing Martha. She couldn't catch her breath. I jumped in the pool and pushed them away, but they started doing the same thing to me. My sister and I got out of the pool because it was time to go home. I went to the shower house to get my clothes and the two boys that were teasing my sister walked in and started pushing me around. I got so mad I started crying, and then I started swinging. I was doing my best, but it wasn't good enough. My sister sent a school friend in to see what was taking me so long. He stopped the fight and told me to leave. My sisters were waiting for me. I didn't stick around to see what was going to happen, but I could hear it. On the way home, I told my mom the story. She turned the car around and went back to the pool, but the boys were gone. After that day my mother decided to enroll me into the Sheriff's Boys Boxing School. That's where I learned how to defend myself and protect my sisters when needed. I don't think I liked boxing because I was so little; I didn't weigh more than sixty pounds soaking wet.

Me and my dog named Red

Chapter 9

Snakes and More Snakes

Moving time—out to the desert by China Lake Naval Weapon Center, which was in the Mojave Desert by Death Valley, California. That's where I met my friend Billy. He and I were two weeks apart in age. We lived in the same park, and we walked to school together every morning. We ended up doing just about everything else together.

One day on our way home, we found a closed box. When we opened it, we found six newborn puppies. All of them were dead. Billy and I buried them and said a little prayer over them.

Billy and I were always trying find things to do. We decided to make some bows and started playing cowboys and Indians. One day, we went to the playground where a couple of girls were playing in the swings. Stupidly, I pointed my bow at them and told them to get out or I would shoot them. I was only ten years old, but I'm not making any excuses for what I did. This is what happens when you're not thinking straight or can't think fast enough. The bowstring slipped from my finger and the arrow went flying. I remember screaming "Move!" but it was too late. The arrow hit one of the girls over her left eye. Thank God it wasn't any lower because it could have killed her. I dropped my bow and ran. I hid in the trees for a long time until I heard my mother calling me. I was so scared. I knew I had killed that little girl. Mom told me the little girl was all right and took me home. I learned a hard lesson that day.

The next day, Mom took me to the little girl's house so I could apologize. I just stood there crying, saying, "I'm so sorry! I'm so sorry!" I thank the good Lord she was all right.

I realize now that I punished myself over the years because of all the bad things I thought I'd done, what I did do to others and for the bad choices I made. My life was so messed up. I think it was the confusion and not being able to concentrate. Sometimes I just couldn't stand looking at myself in the mirror. When I was raped at the age of seven, I thought it was my fault. I've always thought I did something to cause things like that to happen. Whenever I've tried to talk to anyone about my past, they'd tell me how their life was worse, or they'd tell me how stupid I was for thinking the way I did.

Unless someone's walked in my shoes, they wouldn't have the slightest idea what it's like living with ADD. Not even my brother and sisters could understand what I was going through. I know there are a many people who have had far worse challenges. I'm not complaining about my life in that way. I just wanted to understand why I couldn't cope like other people. I would look to others for help, but they would just say I was just a spoiled little brat. My mother was the only one I could turn to for help. She always tried to help me, no matter what my problem was. I don't know why I did the things I did. It's like I didn't have any control over myself.

We moved again, back to Ventura, California. After a short time, we moved back to Ridgecrest. Ridgecrest is the town by the main gate of China Lake. This time, we moved to Wherry Housing outside the back gate of the base. My mother went to work in Ridgecrest at Western Auto, where she stayed for eight years.

One year, Mom asked me what I wanted for Christmas, and I told her I wanted an electric guitar. She bought an acoustic "Mickey Mouse" guitar from my cousin for $5. She said, "If you can teach yourself to play this guitar in a year, I'll buy you that electric guitar."

She saved her pennies while she listened to me trying to play that guitar just about every day after school. I practiced for hours. I slowly learned chords and taught myself how to sing. I always sang with my mother. She has a beautiful voice. Music was the one thing in my life where I could concentrate. I found out my dad knew how to play guitar. Later, he told me he played music with "The Riders of The Purple Sage." He said he worked with The Maddox Brothers and Rose a few times in his life. My dad never wanted me to play music because he said that it was a hard way to make a living. My mother had talked him into helping me on the guitar whenever he had some time, which wasn't very often. Now and then, he taught me a chord or two. I learned the rest on my own. Mom heard me playing and singing as she walked by my room one day. That was the day she knew she'd be buying me an electric guitar. That Christmas, she presented me with a red True Tone electric guitar! That was the best Christmas present ever!

Playing music kept me out of trouble, except for one day on the school bus. I overheard one of the boys telling some of the other kids there was going to be a fight when we got off the bus. I must have had the kind of face that screamed, "I want to be punched!"

All the way home, this guy was calling me names and throwing things at me on the bus. I heard him tell his friends he was going to beat me up when I got off the bus. I didn't even know the kid. He and his friends followed me when I got off the bus. As I walked by one of the houses, he came up behind me and pushed me into the side of the house. I dropped my books, and as I bent down to pick them up, he laughed at me. When I stood up, I came up swinging. The fight moved out into the street, and of course, everyone made a circle around us. I started doing what I was taught in the boxing school. Like a prize fighter, I kept moving so he couldn't hit me. Even though I knew how to fight, I was taught not to unless I had no choice. I heard one of his friends say, "Hey, Mike, I thought you were going to kick his butt?" Mike stopped for a split second and looked over at his friend and said, "I would if he would just stand still." That was my cue. Down he went. I guess the fight was over because he got up and walked away. I could hear his friends laughing. After that day, we became good friends—imagine that.

Most of the kids I went to school with lived in the housing tract where I lived. Jimmy and Larry lived across the street from me, and we'd have water balloon fights at night. One night, we were having our usual who-can-soak-who fight. I was on top of Larry's house, and I was tossing water balloons out in the street. I wasn't watching where I was throwing them, and I hit the side window of a patrol car passing by. Unfortunately, it was in the middle of the summer and the officer had his window down. He got soaked. The good news is, he never knew who threw it, and he couldn't find me.

Some friends and I decided to make some stilts and walk up and down the street. That was a blast. We took playing cards and a clothespin and attach them to our bikes on the spokes. It made it sound like kind of like a motorcycle. At least we thought so.

My friends and I would go around in the summer and mow lawns and clean up people's yards for our money. When I was digging by the side of our house one day, I uncovered a copper bowl. I remember it had Chinese dragons all over the inside and you could see hammer marks on the outside. I sold it to a friend of the family for twenty dollars. I always wondered what it was worth.

We'd go out in the desert for hours and catch snakes and lizards of all kinds. Now and then we would go to Bakersfield, California, to see my aunt and uncle. They had three girls—Peggy, Donna, and Debbie. Peggy was the same as my older sister, and Donna was the same age as my middle sister Martha, and Debbie was a little younger than me. They were close to the same ages as my sisters and me. Every time we'd visit, our parents would go dancing at the Black Board—the club where Buck Owens got his start.

One night after our parents left, my cousins and my sisters decided they wanted to go out running around. They told me I had to stay home with Debbie. I had other plans, and they didn't include staying with my younger cousin. As the girls got in the car and started to leave, I ran out and grabbed the door handle where Peggy was sitting. I wasn't about to let go because I knew they would leave me behind. Peggy said, "Fine, give me your hand, and I'll pull you through the window." Instead, she grabbed my arm and rolled up the window with my arm inside. This is when I learned how to run next to a car because they took off and I either ran or I would have been dragged. Everyone in the car was laughing, and Donna laughed so hard she wet her pants.

I was used to this kind of treatment. Martha would give me a plane ride on the lawn. If you don't know what a plane ride is, it's when a person grabs you by the leg and arm and swings you around in a circle. When my sister got up enough speed, she'd let me go, watching me slide across the lawn like a flat rock. It's a wonder I lived through being a child. But I love my family, no matter how we grew up.

Wherry Housing off base. I was twelve years old.

Chapter 10

Murray Junior High

My cousin and I attended Murray Junior High, grades 6 through 8. When I was in the sixth grade, he was in the eighth. He had a reputation for fighting and getting into trouble. Most of the kids in school were afraid of him, and some even called him a bully behind his back. We had our lunch at the same time. One day at lunchtime, he told me that one of the other eighth graders was telling everyone he was going to beat me up after school. "Don't wait until the end of school," my cousin said. "Go and get it over with now or everyone will think you're afraid of him."

I wanted kids to look up to me and not think I could be bullied. I really didn't want to hurt anyone, but I didn't want to disappoint anyone either. I walked over and punched the boy in the nose. That was it, I thought. The fight ended right there. A few days later two brothers followed me out the back door of the lunchroom. They stopped me on the stairs and said, "Don't think you're going to get away with starting a fight with our friend and walk away just like that."

I tried to explain what had happened, but they were bound and determined to kick my butt. That's when I found out that the boy I hit never said a word about me;

he didn't even know who I was until then. My cousin just wanted to see if I knew how to fight. I always looked up to my cousin, but after what he did that day, I had a hard time trusting him.

I fought the brothers one at a time and won, even though there are no winners in a fight. I was sent to the office, so I didn't win after all. After that, the kids in school left me alone.

One day in History class, I got frustrated because I couldn't understand what the teacher was talking about. He repeated what he said three or four times, but I still couldn't understand what he was trying to say. He grabbed me by the arm after class, took me into another room, and proceeded to give me three swats with a paddle. He told me I was getting the swats because I was being a sarcastic in class and wouldn't listen. I tried to tell him I was having trouble understanding him, but he was determined to try out his golf swing on my bottom.

When I got home from school, I called my mother at work and told her what he had done. She went straight to the school to find out why her son was being physically abused. The principal told her that I wasn't paying attention in class and was distracting the other children. My mother came down on him like a thousand-pound weight! That teacher never touched me again.

I was always getting in trouble for something. After school, I'd go out in the desert and catch all kinds of snakes and lizards and bring them home. My mother would say "Get those darn snakes out of the house!" I loved playing with snakes. I liked to see how quick I was when they struck at me.

I was by myself most of the time growing up. I guess you could say it caused me to become a loner.

During this time in my life, I had few friends—just a couple who lived nearby. I found it hard to be around other kids. I was a little slower-thinking than my friends were, and they'd tease me. That was probably why I got into so many fights growing up. I didn't like being teased, and knowing that, my friends teased me anyway. The older I got, the more I couldn't cope with things. I never liked school very much because I had trouble concentrating, which made it difficult for me to learn.

I remember the first time I got into a fight at school. I was in sixth grade. I was outside playing on the monkey bars, hanging from my knees. Suddenly, a tall kid was standing in front of me with his head sticking through the bars. He looked straight at me. "Get off my bars!" he yelled.

I dropped down to the ground and looked up at him. He stared down at me and said, "Stay off my bars!" As he walked away, I ran up behind him and kicked him in the back of the leg. When he turned around, I hit him in the gut. Right away, I knew I was in trouble when he looked down at me and laughed. Remembering what I learned in boxing school, I decided to take care of this giant.

My first mistake was hitting him again. He just stood there and laughed. He grabbed me and pushed me down on the ground and sat on me. When I looked up, all I could see was his fist doubled up, coming my way. Thankfully, one of the teachers came out and broke it up. Somehow, I knew this first fight would not be my last. Every time I saw this big kid coming my way, I gave him a wide berth.

When I was in the seventh grade, I went into the lunchroom and heard a couple of kids calling a big kid names and saw them making fun of his height. I walked over to them, pushed one kid down in his chair, and said, "You pick on him, you pick on me."

That big kid's name was Mike, and we became great friends after that day. I learned a big lesson that day. No matter what you may think about your life, there is always someone around the corner who is going through just as much, if not more.

One of my teachers made us hold our hands out, smacking them with a ruler when we talked or didn't get our homework done on time. My hands were always red. I really didn't understand why I couldn't learn like all the other kids. My attention deficit disorder was the reason for my confusion. Back then, no one knew what ADD was. It was assumed that the child was lazy and didn't want to learn. You can't imagine how frustrating things were for me and other kids like me—feeling we didn't belong anywhere in this world.

In my opinion, some kids try to commit suicide because they can't cope with the way they are treated. I sometimes considered taking my own life. But then I'd think about my mother and what it would do to her. So I kept pushing on, asking the same question—where do I belong in this world?

Chapter 11

My First Real Date

I was thirteen the first time I got up enough courage to ask a girl out on a date. Her name was Sally, and at the time, I thought I was madly in love with her. I asked her if she would meet me at the theater on base one weekend, and she said she would love to. Even though I thought she was too classy for me, I really liked her a lot. Another problem was that her friends didn't like me. Saturday came around, and it was time to meet her at the movies and we could finally be together. I wore my favorite shirt and splashed on some cologne. I was nervous and excited at the same time. I lived twelve blocks from the theater and ran half the way there!

When I got to the theater, I found some of her friends and asked, "Where's Sally?" They proceeded to tell me that I wasn't good enough for her and she didn't want to be seen with such a nerd like me. They told me to stay away from her. Wham! You could have hit me on the head with a hammer, and it wouldn't have hurt as much. I left the theater and walked back home, crying most of the way. I remember feeling sick to my stomach, and the same question kept coming up. Why me, and what did I do?

I didn't even want to look at myself in the mirror. I couldn't figure out why my heart hurt so much all the time. I felt like I didn't really want to live anymore. I knew back then there was something wrong with me because I had a hard time controlling my thoughts. I got to the point where I hated everyone I saw. I felt like my insides were on fire, and my mind would go berserk. I couldn't think straight. I would find someplace to sit where I could be alone. I'd cry and pound my head, trying to figure out what I did to make people hate me so much. Why was I so different than all the other kids in my school?

My difficulty understanding what the teachers were talking about led me to ask a lot of questions. In turn, the kids in my class laughed at me and made fun of me for it. My teeth were pretty messed up after the accidents I had when I was younger—running into the table and falling out of the tree—and the kids called me Crusader Rabbit and Bucky Beaver. That's when I began staying away from the other kids, becoming even more of a loner. I felt angry and hated myself. I started sneaking out of the house at night, walking the streets alone.

Chapter 12

Catch Me If You Can

On weekends, I'd go over to the base pool and go swimming. One day, I was showering after swimming, getting ready to go home. I was the only one in the shower at the time. I was putting my clothes on when two guys walked in and started pushing me around. They were in their late teens or early twenties—a lot older than I was. One of the guys grabbed and tried to hold me down while the other started taking his pants off. I knew what would happen if I didn't get away. I had been there before. He told his friend to hold me still. I broke loose and started screaming at them, and they let me go and left the shower. When I got outside, I found a police officer and told him what happened. I told him what they were wearing. He left me and went looking for them. I don't know if he ever found them. After that day, I stopped going to the pool. I was afraid something might happen, and I didn't want to take any chances.

About a year later, I was at party with my friends when I found out who one of the guys was. We were sitting around telling jokes and laughing, and lo and behold, guess who walked through the door? It was the younger of the two guys at the pool. I told my friends a little about what happened that day, and the longer I sat there the madder I got. I invited him to go outside with me. He didn't remember who I was, so I kindly reminded him about that day. He remembered and said they were just playing around. I looked at him and said, "So am I!" I knocked him to the ground and the fight was over. I felt pretty good about myself after that night, and that's when I started fighting my way through life. But after a while, I didn't like hurting people, no matter what they did. After every fight I had gotten into, I felt bad for the person I was fighting. I tried to keep my temper under control and not fight unless I had no choice.

Chapter 13
_____

First Band

At the age of fifteen, I started playing rhythm guitar and singing in bands—and again I got in trouble. I played in a band with some friends from school who lived on the base. One night at practice, Larry, the lead guitar player, gave me a guitar he told me he'd rebuilt and painted. I didn't know the guitar was stolen until the police came over to my house asking me questions about it. Larry told them when they came looking for the guitar that I had it at my house and didn't tell them I was not involved. I was so mad at Larry! I gave the guitar to the officers and told them the truth. I called Larry after they left and told him they were coming to pick him up. Larry's dad had to pay for the guitar, but I don't think Larry got in trouble for it because his dad worked for the police department on base.

Our band stayed together for a while longer and his dad drove us to our gigs. On weekends, he'd load us up in his jeep and we'd take the back roads across the desert, looking for artifacts. On one of our trips, we went to an old ghost town off the beaten path. Larry and I were running down a hill and I tripped over something sticking up out of the ground. I went to see what it was. It was covered up except for a corner that was sticking out. I started moving the dirt away and the more I moved, the bigger my eyes got. It was black and had writing on the front in gold letters. It was an old safe. I hollered out for Larry's dad to come over and check it out. We didn't have a shovel or anything else to dig with—it was too deep in the ground to dig out anyway. We marked the place, planning to come back later and dig it up. When we went back the following weekend, someone had beaten us to it. There are a lot of neat things out in the desert to find if you know the right places to look.

My niece Kathy and me. I was fifteen.

Chapter 14

Ghost Towns and Mine Shafts

There are ghost towns all over Kern County. Some of the towns were buried in an earthquake a long time ago, others are still standing, like Keynot and Beveridge. Both were hidden in the Sierra and Nevada Mountains outside of Bishop, California. Believe me, they are hard to find.

I went hiking in the back country with some of my friends out of Bishop, California. One of my friends was standing on the side of a hill, when suddenly he disappeared! The ground gave way under him—it was the roof of an old house. Luckily, he was shaken up a bit but didn't get hurt when he fell through.

When we dropped down inside, it was dark, but we could see enough to find something to light. I couldn't believe what we found. Dishes were still on the table and on the shelves—clothes in the closet—and an old pair of women's lace up boots sitting by a rocking chair. Whoever lived there must have left in a big hurry! We found peaks of other buildings, but we didn't have the right tools to break through to them.

We researched and found out the name of the town and what had happened to it. In the 1800s, a big earthquake destroyed the entire town. The mountain came down upon them without warning. We learned there were few survivors and that they could never find their town again. A few people like us have found the town by accident, but there are no roads or trails to show you the way in.

I've gone on many adventures like that. I loved exploring different places—caves or mine shafts—walking the desert in search of interesting things.

Once I found a mine shaft so old that I had to really watch my step going down the ladder leading into it. I knew there must be all kinds of things down there, like snakes and bats. When I got halfway down, I couldn't see the bottom. I knew it must be very deep because it took me almost thirty minutes to get to where I was, and I wasn't even close to the bottom. There were tunnels going in different directions, so I stepped off the ladder and took one of them. You must watch what you're doing because there can be harmful gasses in some of the caves. As I was walking, I found a weird animal skeleton, at least I think it was an animal. It had wings like a bird, but it was covered with hair-like fur like a rat, and it had bird feet. I took a mental picture of it so I could tell someone about it.

As I went around one of the corners, I got the shock of my life. There were two human skeletons leaning against the wall. Their clothes were nothing but rags. It didn't take me as long to get out as it took me to get in!

I went to the sheriff's office to tell them what I found. They asked me where it was, so I took them back to the place. I waited up top while they went down to investigate. They cheated because they used ropes and a hoist; I had to climb the old ladder. They brought the skeletons back up and put them in bags. I found out later they were two Indians who must have gone down to either get out of the heat or the cold and died there.

Chapter 15

Louisiana Kid

In my second year of high school, I met Don. He just transferred from New Orleans, Louisiana. I noticed him because he was always alone, like me. Don was high strung and would shake when he got nervous or mad. I walked over and introduced myself to him. In that moment, I knew I had met a kindred spirit. We began hanging out together, in search of adventure.

Don and I heard about a place out in the desert that was supposed to be haunted. We decided to go out and try to find it. We took our rifles with us just in case we ran across something else. When we found the place, it was around 5:00 p.m. and getting dark, but we still had enough daylight to see.

It was an old shack and the back part of it was a cave leading to another part of the shack. As we started walking into the cave, Don let out a yell, "Aiyee!" that echoed through the cave.

Halfway through, we could hear heavy footsteps coming in our direction. I looked at Don and said, "What the heck was that?"

Don looked at me and said, "I'm not going to stick around to find out!"

Being from Baton Rouge, Louisiana, you can imagine his accent. I shouted out, "Whoever you are, we have guns and we're not afraid to use them!"

Whatever it was, it was so close we could hear it breathing. It stopped for a minute then started to walk a little faster. That's how we knew it wasn't an animal. It had to be something bigger. It got deadly quiet for a couple of minutes, and then we heard footsteps again, this time faster. Don and I looked at each other and started running for the car. I tripped over a piece of tin and Don kept running. I turned and fired off a couple of rounds and got to my feet.

I made it to the car just as Don was pulling away. I couldn't believe it! He was going to leave me there! I yelled at him, he stopped the car, and I jumped in. Don looked like he had seen a ghost. I looked at him and said, "You were going to leave me behind!"

Don answered, "No, I was just moving the car down the road."

We were both quiet on the way home. After Don dropped me off at my house, I didn't talk to him for a week.

Chapter 16

The Psychedelic Wheels

My family moved into town on Reeves Street in a house my mother bought. My uncle would come over from Bakersfield on the weekends and work on the house. They knocked out the living room wall to make it bigger. The add-on was made of brick. He even built a nice fireplace in the corner.

I met some kids who lived close by my house. Our place was right across the street from a trailer park. I put a small band together with some of my school friends that we called "The Psychedelic Wheels."

We practiced in my garage and girls started coming around to listen. I started seeing one of the girls. Her name was Ann. Ann's parents were from another country, and they didn't like the idea of their daughter hanging out with me or any other boy. They didn't understand English well, so Ann had to translate when she introduced me to them. I could tell they didn't want me to be hanging around with their little girl. We were boyfriend and girlfriend anyway.

My band practiced at the bass player's house in his backyard now and then. His mom and dad loved it because we were playing a lot of old standard country music. We'd practice somewhere every day after school. We began playing at teen dances in town, on the base and at the Elks Lodge. One weekend, we heard they were having a battle of the bands contest at the Elks Lodge, so we decided to enter. I felt we had one of the best bands in town. We competed with three other bands.

We came in second place, but later that day we found out that one of the mothers of the other band members was caught taking tickets out of our coffee can and putting them into her son's. It was too late to say anything, and it was their word against ours. Sometime after that, our band broke up, and the guys went their own ways.

My mom and dad would go to the Moose Lodge to dance on weekends. My mother knew the band and asked if I could come down and sing with them a couple of times. They said, "We don't see why not, but he'll have to stay outside on the breaks." I was only sixteen at the time. When I sang with the band the first time, the band members acted like I was a star. They didn't know how that voice came out of me. The customers liked me so much that the club hired me to sing with the band every Saturday night. I guess you could say that's where I got my start. Sixteen years old and already a star—at least I felt like one at the time. I worked there for about a year until the band broke up. I stopped playing for a while because I was still in school, and I couldn't do both.

Tony and David and Billy and me

Chapter 17

Troll Hunting

On weekends, the kids in town would hang out at the A&W Root Beer stand in town. It was cool to go there and see all the people you knew, like watching *American Graffiti* all over again. All the parties would start there.

One night, we were sitting around trying to think of something to do. One of the older boys started talking about some trolls he saw out at the old airport outside of Inyokern. We all decided to jump in our cars and go troll hunting. I knew there wasn't any such thing, but I went along for the fun. All the way out there, everyone was talking about the trolls and what they looked like. When we arrived at the airport, we bailed out of the cars and started running around yelling for trolls. I don't think anyone was even thinking about the snakes that were out there. They were having too much fun trying to scare each other. One of the older boys yelled that they had caught a troll in one of the bunkers. Everyone ran to the bunker to see the amazing catch, but when we got there the only thing in the bunker was a dead rabbit someone had stuffed halfway in one of the air shafts. They told everyone the troll had gotten away and everybody believed them.

The fun stopped when a loud scream came from one of the cars. Apparently, one of the younger girls said a troll was trying to get in the car. When we got there, we found big scratch marks where it looked like something tried to open the door. Everyone started to panic, running around looking for the troll. I got tired of it all and decided to hitch a ride back to town. That night was talked about for years to come.

Chapter 18

The Cemetery

One night, Don and I decided to play a trick on some of our friends, so we took them out to the cemetery for bedtime stories. We had one of our friends dress up and meet us there to scare some girls. It was around midnight, and I told him I would give him a signal when to walk up to the car and plant his face against the window. It all went perfectly to plan. After it was over and we were laughing about it, suddenly someone wearing a mask walked up and planted their face against the driver's window and started rocking the car. I looked at Don and said, "Who the hell was that?"

After the panic stopped, we got out of the car to find out who it was, but he had already gone. We never found out who that masked man was. It didn't stop us from doing it again!

Looking back to when we were kids, we came up with some of the craziest stunts to do for fun. I never believed what other people told me about things—I had to find out myself. Like trolls and ghosts, it was all just a game. Every weekend, there was a party somewhere and free beer.

Back then, we walked just about everywhere we wanted to go until Don got his driver's license. But most of the time, we had to walk. We'd walk out to the drive-in theater and sneak over the fence. We could always find someone to sit with. I started drinking at an early age. I felt like it was the only way I could cope with what life had dealt me. I can't tell you what movies were playing those nights at the drive-in.

Chapter 19

Desert War Games

Don and I got bored one day and decided to go out in the mountains close to town with our .22 rifles and play some war games. Hiding in the rocks and shooting close to each other, luckily no one got hurt. One day, we broke into a mining shack and borrowed a couple of sticks of dynamite. We set the sticks up and shot at them, trying to blow them up, but nothing ever happened. We thought that was fun, as stupid as it was. We figured we didn't have much going for us at the time and really didn't care. One day after being up in the foothills, Don and I were walking back home when I heard a gunshot, and the dust flew next to my right foot. I looked at Don and we started running.

That night, we were walking to Don's house when an old man walked out of the alley and said, "I'm going to get you. I'm going to get both of you!" I stood my ground. When I turned to say something to Don, he had already taken off running and left me standing there with my fist doubled, ready to fight. After a few minutes, the old man turned and walked away.

I went straight to Don's. "Where the heck did you go? You left me standing there alone!"

Don said, "I had to go to the bathroom."

I just looked at him, laughed, and said, "I was ready to fight the old goat."

Don answered, "Not me." I was the one that always did all the fighting, not Don.

I never once saw Don fight, but he certainly started a lot of them—and I had to finish them. After that night, we started watching our backs when we were out.

Don had trouble coping with life. He had a serious nervous condition, and he was always hyper. He told me people were out to get him. He never trusted anyone.

I didn't know too much about Don's past before he moved to Ridgecrest, only that he came from Louisiana with his mother. When he talked to people, he was short with them. He acted like he was mad all the time. When we went to some of the dances in town, he was rude to the other kids. One night, we went to a teen dance on base. When Don asked one of the girls to dance and she turned him down, he got angry. "Let's get out of here," he said.

When I asked him what was wrong, he said, "These girls think they're better than me."

"So ask someone else," I said.

We ended up leaving, like always because Don was trying to start fights with anyone and everyone.

I missed out on lots of things back then trying to keep Don out of trouble. I pulled him out of so many jams I lost count. I don't know why I hung around with him for such a long time. I guess I felt sorry for him because he didn't have any other friends. I really didn't have many friends myself, and it made me stand back and take a good look at myself.

Once Don and I got involved with black magic and witchcraft. It all began when I bought a book called *The Satanic Bible*. I looked at it as a joke. I didn't realize Don took it seriously until he started doing things that the book described. One night, we were driving down one of the streets in town. "The Holy Bible" book was in the back seat of his mother's car. He started ranting about Satan and God. He stopped the car, grabbed the Bible from the back seat, and said, "This is what I think of The Bible." He started ripping the pages out of it.

"Have you lost your mind?" I yelled. "You really are crazy. What are you doing?"

"I'm giving my soul to Satan so I can have everything I've ever wanted," he answered.

That was the straw that broke the camel's back—and all four legs. I'd had enough. I told him he was crazy and that he had finally lost it. "Don, just drop me off at the store around the corner and I'll walk home.

That was the wrong thing to say and the wrong time to say it. Don hit the gas and off we went. We were on a straight road to the next town, about nine miles from home. I looked over and he was doing close to 95 mph. I think that's as fast as his mother's car would go. In a calm voice I said, "If you really want to kill us, we should get some beer first and have some fun on the way out. Where we're going, they don't sell beer."

He started laughing and slowed the car down to the speed limit. We got back in town and stopped at one of the stores to find someone who would buy us some beer. Don looked over at me and said, "That really didn't scare you, did it?" I wasn't about to tell him the truth.

We couldn't find anyone to buy us beer, so we decided to call it a night. Don dropped me off at my house. After he drove away, I stood outside for about a half an hour before I went in. I was debating whether I should end this friendship. It felt like it was going downhill fast.

Chapter 20

In Trouble with the Law

A couple of days later, Don and I were walking down a street in town when three guys jumped us. The fight was on. Don wasn't much of a fighter, so I did most of the fighting. Just as the battle started getting good, the police pulled up. The other guy told the police officers I had pulled a knife on them and started the fight. The officers believed them and took Don and me to the police station. The officers didn't like either Don or me and one of them said, "You two are always causing trouble," which was not the truth. It just happened that one of the officers who picked us up was the same one who had started a fight with my brother in his office a while back. My brother worked as a police officer, and he got into a heated discussion in his office. Push came to shove, and my brother broke his favorite watch. I reminded the officer of who I was and who my brother was. The officer said, "You're just like your brother, always causing trouble." That was the wrong thing to say to me. My brother never caused trouble with anyone in his entire life; it wasn't his way.

They took us to the police station and called our parents. My mother came to pick me up. When she asked me what had happened, I told her the truth. I never fought unless I didn't have a choice, and she knew that. I didn't have a knife, and I never carried one.

I went to work at the fair when it came to town, setting up the rides and the tents during the day. That first night, Don and I went to the fair to hang out and have some fun. I had a blast just walking around, checking things out and trying to meet girls.

Another night, Don and I were walking around the fairgrounds and ran into some of the guys from school who weren't too crazy about Don. When they started making snide remarks about his accent, he got mad and said, "I'm going to beat up one of you boys if you don't leave us alone." What he meant was, I was going to do it for him. I just stood there watching and waiting. They finally left us alone.

It was getting late, so we started walking home. We always took the shortest way across the desert—but this time, we had some company. The guys we had trouble with were following us. I told Don, "Just keep walking and don't say anything."

As they got closer to us, I could hear them calling both of us names, like "chicken" and "little girls." That made me mad, so I stopped and let them catch up with us. I turned around and said, "Do you guys have a problem with me?"

One of them said, "Yes, you're in our way."

"What do you mean, I'm in your way?" I replied.

"Our beef is with Don, not you."

"If you want Don, you'll have to go through me first," I answered. I looked at Don, and he knew what was coming. There were three of them around our age. I looked at the biggest boy and said, "If I'm in your way, move me!"

He stood there for a minute, looked at the other two boys, and said, "Let's go. It's not worth it."

They turned and walked away.

After they left, Don said "Are you crazy? They would have stomped our butts!"

I said, "Maybe yours, but I can guarantee they would have had a hard time kicking mine." They would have had a fight on their hands when it came to me.

I had been practicing martial arts for some time, and I wasn't afraid of anyone now. All the way home, I heard from him what he would have done to them, and I just laughed. Again, it made me stand back and take a good look at our friendship. I truly didn't like to fight, but I guess that's how I chose to prove myself to everyone back then. Now I realize it was a waste of time.

Several days later, we were walking downtown when a couple of guys decided they didn't like the way we looked at them. We were in one of the back alleys, taking our usual shortcut. One of them started pushing Don into the wall. "Why can't you just leave us alone?" I asked.

The guy turned around and told me, "Stay out of it— it isn't your fight."

The one standing in front of me started pushing me back toward the other wall. I figured I had no choice, so I started swinging. When I knocked him down, his buddy came over to see if he was all right. Then I started pounding on him. The next thing I knew, Don was pulling me off the guy.

A few weeks later, Don and I were at a local hangout. Guess who pulled in beside us. Yep! The police officer from the station, who was now off duty. He got out of his car and went inside. When he came back out, Don and I were leaning against the front of Don's car. I looked at the guy and said, "How brave are you now?"

He put his drink down on the hood of his car, went around to the back, popped open his trunk, and pulled out a shovel. He looked at me and said, "Come on if you think you're so bad."

I just looked at him and laughed. He said, "Yeah, I thought so—all talk and no walk."

When he put the shovel back in the trunk and shut the lid, he wasn't fast enough. I only hit him once, and he went down. I said, "Come on, get up."

He put his hand up and said he'd had enough. I turned and walked away. That was the last I saw of him.

Chapter 21

Charlie Manson

Don and I decided to take a short trip to Trona, about twenty-five miles away. When we got there, we met a couple of girls at a hamburger stand. They asked us if we wanted to go to a party with them. I answered, "Sure, where's the party?"

"Out at Charlie's place," one of the girls said, "in the foothills."

They were strange girls; they each had an upside down cross tattooed in the middle of their foreheads. They gave us directions on how to get there. It was supposed to be a small ranch on the outskirts of town. It was about 6:30 p.m. and around ninety-five degrees by the time we arrived. It reminded me of one of those love-in's you'd see on TV in the sixties. When we arrived, people were walking around looking like zombies. Most of the girls had the same cross tattoo on their forehead between their eyes.

We asked one of the guys if this is where the party was. He said, "Party? Every day is a party." Then he handed Don a joint and said, "Party on, bro."

Neither of us ever smoked dope, but Don kept it in case one of the girls wanted it. Don and I saw a girl we knew from school. She was wondering what we were doing out there. We told her that we heard there was a big party out here. She told us we couldn't stay unless Charlie said we could.

I said, "Don, I think we should go. This doesn't feel right."

Don told me I was just paranoid because everyone was doing some sort of drugs. The girl from school told us she would introduce us to Charlie. "Who the heck is Charlie?" I asked.

She took us to a big tree where there were five or six people sitting around smoking dope. Some of them looked like they were going to pass out. Well, we met Charlie. Boy, what a freak! When she introduced us, this guy stared at us like we weren't even there. I put my hand out to shake his, but he just kept staring at me. He gave me the willies! I told Don, "I'm leaving, even if I have to walk all the way back home."

Don said, "Okay, we'll go in just a minute. I want to look around a little bit more."

I was getting mad by this time. Don was just looking for somebody to party with. We walked up to some girls and asked if they wanted to get out of there and go somewhere else.

One of the girls said, "We belong to Charlie, so you'll have to ask him if it's okay."

I said to Don, "That's it! I'm out of here!"

On the way back to the car, we met Charlie again and he said "You can't tell anyone about this place. You won't, will you?"

To me, it sounded like a threat, so Don and I left.

We talked about it all the way back to town. Later we saw the girl who was at the party and asked her what was going on with all those girls at Charlie's place. She said, "He takes care of them. If they don't have a place to stay, they can stay with Charlie for free and get all the drugs they want."

When I asked her about the crosses on their foreheads, she told me it was an upside-down cross. Now I knew they were crazy. It wasn't until a few weeks later I found out who Charlie was—Charles Manson! That was scary. When I told Don, he just looked at me the way Charles did. I just about kicked him in the butt. I said, "That wasn't a bit funny." He just laughed.

Chapter 22

Boys Will Be Boys

One of my best friends and lead player in one of my bands was Tony. My friend Billy and I met him at our local haunt, and he told us about a kid who was pushing him around, trying to start a fight. Tony wasn't a fighter. I asked him who the guy was. Tony said, "His name is Johnny T."

I found Johnny T downtown with a bunch of his friends. I pretended I was one of his best friends, and we started talking about the fight between him and Tony. He started bragging about how Tony wouldn't fight him. He said, "Tony is a little cry baby, so I kicked the crap out of him anyway."

The more I listened, the madder I got. The more he talked, the more my blood boiled. Billy and I walked Johnny T to his house to keep up the pretense of being friends. We got as far as the water tank down the street when I couldn't take any more of this kid's bragging.

I said, "You must think you're pretty tough. I could probably kick your butt with one hand tied behind my back.

When I turned around, Johnny T already had his fists up and was ready to fight me. With one hit, he was out like a light. It was the first time I had ever knocked someone out, and it scared the heck out of me. After we helped him to his feet, we walked him over to where he lived because I wanted to make sure he was okay. Billy and I went to my house. Billy and I never let anyone know what happened that night, not even Tony.

Billy's cousin, Mike, me, and Billy were all close. Mike lived next door to a factory where they built coffins. One night, we decided to sneak in through one of the windows and run around for a while.

It was a small building, and there were about twenty-five coffins inside. We were trying to scare each other, kind of like a game of hide-and-seek. I crawled inside one of the coffins to scare Billy. About the time I got inside, Mike walked by looking for us. He was standing right next to where I was hiding, and I couldn't resist the opportunity. I reached out and grabbed Mike by the shirt and all hell broke loose! He started screaming, and the more he screamed, the harder I laughed. I laughed so hard the coffin I was in fell off the table, and I came rolling out—still laughing.

The three of us would walk around town for hours at night, just talking and laughing. We'd talk about what we wanted to do with our lives when we got older. I think of the three of us, I was the only one who accomplished it.

Chapter 23

Army Days

Mike, Billy, and I decided to join the army together on the buddy plan. Mike and Billy's parents had already signed for them to go in. My mother didn't really want me to go, but she signed the papers anyway. My dad volunteered to take us to Los Angeles to the induction center. It was the first time in my life my father had volunteered to do anything for me. We had to lie when we filled in the paperwork because I wasn't eighteen yet. I was afraid they wouldn't take me because I had curvature of the spine, and it kept me from doing a lot of physical things. I knew if I told them they wouldn't have taken me, so I didn't tell them and they took me in.

We arrived in LA at the Induction Center. After all the paperwork was signed, we were taken to the Lankershim Hotel downtown. This place was a dump, and I could see why. It was full of recruits—army, navy, air force, and marines. People were drinking, smoking pot, throwing things out of their room windows into the streets. There were a lot of guys who were drafted and didn't want to be there.

The next morning, bright and early, buses lined up in front of the hotel to take us to our next destination. Our first stop was Fort Ord, California. It was an all-day trip to the basic training center. It was scary for the three of us because we were the only three who had enlisted. Everyone else had been drafted. We were harassed most of the time that we were there. As soon as the bus stopped, the doors flew open, and a drill sergeant stepped onto the bus. He started yelling at everyone, telling us to get off. He called us ladies, and I remember how boiling mad I was because of the way we were treated.

As I walked pass the drill sergeant, I gave him a dirty look. That was the wrong thing to do. He grabbed me, stuck his face right in mine, and asked me if I thought he was pretty. I said, "No, sir, I don't."

I was never one to think fast, so I said the first thing that came to my mind. His face turned a bright red, and I knew I was in trouble as soon as I stepped off the bus. I don't know how they knew, but there were two more waiting for me outside. They grabbed me, threw me up against the bus, and started yelling. I think they thought I was deaf.

After everyone was off the bus, they told me to get in line. I was so mad I was shaking. After we were all in line, they marched us into the barber shop, and there went my hair. I always took good care of my hair. It was long—down to my shoulders. I looked like a skinned rabbit when they finished with me. Next stop was the clothing: shirts, pants, boots, all the great essentials we would need for the long haul. We were ushered out the back door, down the street for our vaccination shots, and then on to our barracks. Mike was put on a bus and taken to the top of the hill to the new brick barracks. Billy and I were in the old wooden ones at the bottom of the hill. That was the last time I saw

Mike. I never knew what happened to him after that day. So much for the buddy plan. It was great until the papers were signed. Then they put you wherever they wanted.

We went in for testing, and of course, I got a very low score. They stuck me in the infantry. Billy's assignment was clerical work. After the test, they ran us around the PT field with our duffel bags slung over our shoulders. It was heavy just to carry, and they had us trying to run with it. One kid was having trouble trying to keep up with the rest of us. He kept falling to the ground and we tried to help him. One time he fell, one of the drill sergeants walked over and kicked him in the side and told him to get the hell up off the ground. When the kid didn't move, the other drill sergeant went over to check on him, and they called for an ambulance. We heard later the kid died from a punctured lung and a massive heart attack. We never found out any more about it.

We arrived at our barracks and started putting things away when here they came again, mouths blaring. "You have five minutes to get your gear put away, then line up in the street!"

After we were all lined up, the drill sergeant came by for inspection. If we had hair on our faces, they made us dry shave. One of the guys looked like someone had slit his throat. We started double timing it to the armory where they proceeded to give each of us our number for our weapons. This number was to be remembered all through basic training. Everything went so fast it made my head spin. There were times I couldn't remember my own name, much less a number.

The next morning, they came in screaming again. "Get your lazy butts out of my barracks!"

We were back into the street again for roll call and on to the mess hall for some chow. After that we double-timed it back to the armory to pick up our weapons for a long march. When the drill sergeant called out names, we were supposed to yell out our number. I couldn't remember what my number was. The drill sergeant came over, threw me against the wall, and started screaming again, calling me everything in the book. All the time this was going on, my mind was racing. I was so mad that all I could hear were thoughts going through my head—ways to get even with him without getting into trouble. After he finished, he tossed a rifle at me and told me to get in line.

That whole day we marched, then started bayonet training. We were on the PT field learning different ways to use our rifles, then the pongee sticks. These were long sticks with a big ball at the end. The ball was cushioned so when we hit each other it didn't hurt. The sergeant called me out to be his guinea pig because of what had happened back at the armory. What he didn't know was that when we were kids, we would do this with broom handles. When I was in martial arts classes they taught us how to use the staff, which was like pongee sticks. He tried to hit me, but I countered everything he threw at me. It made him so mad he walked over to me and put his stick under my throat and pushed me back in line. It seemed no matter what I did, it was wrong.

The next night, they loaded us up in the Deuce and a half, a big cattle truck, and took us away from the base for war games. I thought this was cool. Our orders where to take the general hostage from one of the tents. As we marched down the road, another platoon ambushed us. I dove behind a big bush, trying to hide. I saw them looking around for the ones they didn't capture and then they left. There were only four of us left. I told the other three to follow me and the four of us would capture the general. As the captured platoon was being marched down the road to the holding tent in camp, we followed them so they couldn't see us. They arrived at their camp, and we held back a little until they got all the prisoners in the tent. We could hear them as they started calling roll call. The four of us sneaked around to the general's tent and waited for him to show up. About twenty minutes later, he came walking through the front door of the tent. Two of us followed him in and the other two came through the back. "GOT YA." It was a perfect capture. There was only one thing wrong. The war games were over, and we weren't told. For the next week the four of us were pulling KP duty. It was at this time I received my orders for Vietnam.

After completing my service, I received an honorable discharge. That was the end of my military career. To this day, I still have nightmares and see the faces of the men in my company who were killed in Vietnam.

When I returned home, my mom and dad were separated. My mother and sisters were living in a small apartment, so I slept on the floor. It didn't take very long for me to get right back into my old routine. I started hanging out with Larry and his brothers once more, and we started playing music again. That's when I met Becky.

Chapter 24

A Family of My Own

A whole new life started for me after Larry and I met. I went to a party out in the desert where I met Becky. Becky and some of her friends were all out drinking. I wasn't with anyone, so Becky and I started hanging out. I invited her to come over to band practice one night at Larry's house. I didn't know we weren't supposed to have guests at practice, so everyone was a little mad at me that night.

I was living in a small apartment downtown at the time, and I asked Becky if she wanted to come over so we could talk and get to know each other better. She didn't have a car, so I drove out to where she lived on the outskirts of town, picked her up at home, and of course, I met her mom. Her stepfather despised me. Later, I found out why.

Becky and I had been dating for about three months when I asked her to marry me. Becky was only sixteen, so her mother had to sign papers giving us permission to marry. Her stepfather was furious. Becky told me the reason her stepfather didn't like me. He was always trying to get in bed with her at night, so she had to put a lock on her door to keep him out. After she told me that, I was furious, wanting to hold him accountable for what he'd done to her. But it was just a thought.

On December 12, 1969, Becky and I were married in the courthouse in Ridgecrest where we lived. Her mother was there and so was my dad. After we married, we honeymooned in Los Angeles and Becky moved into my small apartment. It was barely big enough for the two us.

I lost my job because I took off to get married, so we ended up moving into her mother's three-bedroom house until we could get on our feet. The only problem was that we had to share it with her stepbrother and stepfather. Becky's stepbrother Johnny was a diagnosed psychopath. As soon as we moved in, I went out looking for work and Johnny decided to go snooping around in our bedroom looking for something to steal. He found a set of knives my brother had sent to me from Germany where he was stationed in the army. One was a Bowie knife, and the other was a skinning knife in the same scabbard. Both knives were collectibles made of nickel silver with bone handles carved with elk heads. They were the only things I'd received while my brother was overseas.

When I discovered them missing, I confronted Johnny about it. He denied taking them. A few days later, out behind the house I found the bowie knife. The blade was broken, and the handle shattered. He had been throwing it at a tree. I was so mad I went looking for him. Becky jumped in the car with me, and we saw Johnny walking down a dirt road. I pulled off the road and drove as close as I could to him. I hollered out to him, but he just ignored me, and that made me even madder. I stopped the car and got out; I figured if he wasn't coming to me, I was going to him. As I started walking, I saw him pick up a board from the road. Becky told me to leave him alone. I turned around and said, "Whose side are you on anyway?"

As I got closer, Johnny took off running. I wasn't going to chase him across the desert. I went home and waited for him—I knew he had to come home some time. It was almost dark when he finally showed up. I guess he was waiting for his dad to come home to protected him. When I told his father about the incident, he said, "You should have had them locked up."

I said, "They were in my dresser drawer in our bedroom behind a locked door."

As soon as Johnny walked in the house, I grabbed him, and the fight was on. It didn't last very long. Becky's mom intervened and stopped it. I told Johnny I didn't beat him up because I had a lot of respect for Becky's mother. I turned to Johnny's dad and said, "If you think this is over, you are sadly mistaken.

His dad told me I had better not touch his son. "Touch?" I retorted. "Who said anything about touching?"

I looked over at Becky, and all she said was, "Let it go." I was getting tired of things happening to me, and no one would do anything about it. Well, I let it go for that night, went into our bedroom, and slammed the door behind me. I could hear Johnny and his dad in the living room laughing and my blood started boiling. I came back out into the living room and almost knocked Johnny and his father down when I went past them on my way out the front door.

About a week later, it was Johnny's birthday and his dad bought him a semiautomatic .22 rifle. That was a dumb thing to do! While Johnny and his dad where gone the next day, I went into Johnny's bedroom took his .22. When they came home, Johnny went into his bedroom and came running out screaming, "Where's my .22?"

"What .22?" I said, playing dumb. I asked, "Where did you put it? I haven't the slightest idea what you are talking about."

He said, "You know what I am talking about."

"I haven't seen your toy gun, Johnny." I started laughing.

Then his dad said, "Okay, you can give him back his rifle."

I looked at his dad with a smile on my face and said, "I think he should have had it locked up." I said, "Payback's a bummer, isn't it?" and walked out the door.

It was never mentioned again after that. But it wasn't over between me and Johnny—not by a long shot. After that, Johnny started doing all kinds of crazy stuff to Becky and me.

One day, we got a call that Becky's mother had been taken to the hospital. We rushed over there to find out what had happened. Apparently, she and her husband where sleeping in the living room, and for some reason, the pilot light went out on the furnace right next to them. I thought it was a bit strange that Johnny's bedroom door was shut, and his window was wide open in the middle of the winter. It turned out that Becky's mom was all right, but her stepfather had to stay in the hospital a little longer.

About a month later, they found out that Becky's dad had cancer. He died shortly thereafter. At the funeral home, I was watching Johnny for some sort of reaction. When he walked up to his dad's casket, he had a big smile on his face. I knew in my heart he'd tried to kill them both, but who would believe me?

After a year went by, Becky's mother remarried. Her husband owned a home in town so that's where they lived. Becky and I bought the house out of town and Johnny moved in with Becky's mom. Bad mistake. It was about five months later that Becky's new stepfather passed away. That left Becky's mother with a big two-story house. The house had an upstairs and an unfinished apartment I began working on. After it was done, Becky and I moved in so we could help her mother. Her mother was getting up there in age, so she couldn't do much. She had Becky when she was in her late forties. I put some real good locks on the doors so certain people couldn't get in. The stairway had a separate door from outside, so it had the best locks on it. The first couple of months were fine—not one incident. Then my birthday came around.

Chapter 25

Here's Johnny

I went to the grocery store to pick up a few things. As I was leaving, I heard a gunshot from across the street. I looked over and saw a fellow with another man on the ground. I shut my car door and ran over to help. One man was holding the other one down, yelling for help. The man on the bottom had a pocketknife, trying to slit his own wrist. I grabbed his hand and got the knife away from him. The other guy said, "He just shot the lady in the beauty parlor!"

I asked, "Do you have him?"

He said, "Yes, but check on the lady inside."

As I walked in, all I could see was blood—lots of it. There was a shotgun lying on the floor next to the lady's body. It looked like a .410 shotgun, single shot. He must have walked up behind her while she was getting her hair done and put the gun to the back of her head. Sadly, her sixteen-year-old daughter was right there, waiting for her mother to finish. I went home and told Becky what had happened and why I was so late getting back home.

I decided to sit down at the piano and play a little bit. That's how I got my mind off things. When I started playing, Becky's mom began singing one of the gospel songs she knew. We were all trying to put what happened behind us for a while. All was well until Johnny came home and decided he was going to start some trouble. Up until then, everything had been going well. Johnny walked into the kitchen. The piano was right by the doorway into the kitchen, so I could see Johnny off to my right.

He made some nasty remarks about the way I was playing the piano. I wasn't that great of a piano player, but I tried. I ignored him for as long as I could. Then he turned to Becky's mother and started calling her names. I stopped playing and turned toward the kitchen. Remember the stuff he pulled in the past? I finally had enough. I saw a butcher knife lying on the table that hadn't been there before. I got up from the piano and walked up to Johnny. He was a little shorter than I was and about five years younger. He looked at me and said, "Having a good birthday?" He started laughing and reached for the knife. I came up with a right cross and caught him on the jaw. He spun around and grabbed the knife off the table. He missed the first and second swings. On third swing, I blocked it and hit him with a left. It seemed that my blows weren't affecting him. The fight moved into the living room, and he was swing wildly. He acted like he was on PCP, which I found out later was true. I finally kicked the knife out of his hand. To my surprise, he had another knife stashed inside the couch. He had his back toward me so when I got closer to him, I didn't see the knife until it was too late. As he turned and swung, I stepped back, and he missed. I blocked the second attempt. He turned, jabbed, and cut my right arm and took another swing.

When I stepped back out of the way, I tripped over the coffee table and down I went on my back. When I looked up, Johnny was looming over me, trying to stab me again. I kicked him in the chest, but all it did was slow him down. Suddenly, I heard Becky off to my right screaming at the top of her lungs, "Johnny, if you don't put the knife down, I'm going to shoot you!"

I looked over for just a split second to see that she had my .357 pistol, pointed right at his head. He dropped the knife and out the front door he ran. Becky's mom called the police, but they couldn't find him. Becky was afraid he would return to finish the job.

About a week later, Johnny came back home when we weren't there. He started breaking things in the house. I think he was looking for something he couldn't find. Becky's mom thought someone had broken into the house, but when I told her I saw Johnny walking down the street not too far from the house, we all knew what happened. Becky's mom told us that she found a bag stuffed down by the arm of the recliner. She said she flushed the contents down the toilet. I said, "You should have given it to the police." She just looked at me and said nothing.

After all that happened, Johnny stayed away from the house until he knew we were gone. One night about eleven o'clock, we heard Becky's mom downstairs screaming at someone. I ran downstairs in time to see the backdoor slam shut. She said Johnny came home wanting her to give him some money, and when she refused, he blew up. She said he must have heard us coming down the stairs because he turned and ran out the door.

I didn't wait for her to call the police; I picked up the phone and started dialing. She asked me "Who are you calling?"

I told her, "The police."

"Please don't call them," she begged. "Let him cool off and he'll be all right."

I was getting tired of her protecting him every time he got in trouble, which was quite often. Johnny finally moved out of the house. Everything was peaceful again, but it didn't last long. I was ready to pack up my belongings and leave. Everyone in that family seemed to love all the drama.

Chapter 26

Filled with Demons

I went to work playing music down at one of the clubs in town. Becky's mother was very religious and didn't like the idea of me playing in bars. She always said it was the devil's den and no good could come of it. I told her it was just a job, and she said that didn't matter.

"People drinking, getting drunk, fighting—it's just not right," she said.

I asked her which was worse: me playing in bars or her working for the government building missiles that will destroy people's lives.

"I don't build anything," she said.

"That's my point," I said. "I don't make people drink and party—I'm just there doing my job." I reminded her that Archangel Michael was a musician.

She replied "Yes, and so was the devil."

One night, when I came home from teaching a martial arts class, I walked into one of Becky's mom's Bible studies. She invited me to have a seat and join them. I have always been interested in different religions, so I sat down on the floor next to the wall and started listening to everyone giving their interpretation of the Bible. I decided to throw my two cents' worth in. That was the wrong thing to do. Before the session was over, she had everyone believing I was full of demons. I might have been full of something, but for sure it wasn't demons. Before I left the room, she almost had me believing her.

After all that had happened, I just couldn't take anymore. No one ever did anything about what happened between Johnny and me. Becky and I decided to pack up and move to Ukiah, California, and stay with my mother and her husband for a while.

Chapter 27

The Move to Ukiah

I got a job playing music in Ukiah at the Happiness Is Club the following week. We moved into a spare bedroom in Mom's trailer. Becky was pregnant with our daughter Kelli. I started doing singles on the weekends, but I was only making thirty dollars a night, plus my tips. At the time, I was the only one working, and with Becky pregnant, we needed milk and food. During the day, Mom's husband Rick and I would go to Clear Lake and catch fish for dinner. We'd always come home with enough striped bass to last all week. Rick drove trucks for a living, so there were times Mom and Rick would be gone on the road.

Times got so bad for us I would follow the milkman around to get milk for Becky and the baby. I guess when you get down that low you'll do anything to survive.

My daughter, Kelli Michelle, was born December 9, 1972, in Ukiah. We stayed there until Kelli got a little older. We moved up the road to Blue Lake where I went to work playing bass guitar with a band at the Lake Shore Inn.

I had never played bass in my entire life. Since I played guitar, I knew it couldn't be that hard, so up on the stage I went. I worked there for about five months, until the drummer and the lead player got into a fight in the bar. They fired the drummer. He'd gotten me this job, so I followed him down the street to another bar.

I had a great reputation for singing by then, so it wasn't hard for us to find another gig. We hired a lead player and named our trio The True Notes. We were together for about three months. The club wasn't doing well and expected us to pull them out of the hole. It couldn't be done, so I went to work managing some cabins next to the lake.

One day, the owner of the apartments stopped by and said, "It's great that all the cabins were rented, and the place looks really nice, but I have to let you go." He told me some of his friends were going to take over management. I was angry and felt used again.

Before we packed up and moved out, someone broke into our house and knocked over all the aquariums I kept snakes in. There were snakes everywhere. Since the owner wanted us gone right away, I didn't have time to clean up or mess with the snakes, so I just closed the door and went back to Ridgecrest.

My kids, Sean and Kelli. They were my
world, something I did right!

My beautiful daughter, Kelli

Kelli

My handsome son Sean all grown up

Chapter 28

My Big Surprise

When we got back to Ridgecrest, I left Becky with some friends of ours and asked Larry if he could go back up to Ukiah and help me move the rest of my things we'd left in storage. The night before we left, we had a little coming home party with some of Larry's friends. One of the guys was in the Navy and lived off base with his little brother, who was about sixteen years old.

It was a ten-hour drive to Ukiah, and we were tired when we arrived. The next morning, we packed the truck and back to Ridgecrest we went. It was late when we arrived back at Larry's house. I went into the bedroom where Becky and I were staying, and to my surprise, there was Becky, passed out. A sixteen-year-old-boy was coming out of the room as I was going in. I can't write in this book what was going through my mind at that time.

I left the room and slammed the door behind me. I went to Becky's mother's house where I found my daughter. Becky's mom told me Becky had dropped Kelli off right after I left for Blue Lake. I left Kelli with Becky's mother and went back to Larry's house. When I got there Becky was gone. Suddenly, Larry's father came busting in screaming at me about taking Larry up to Ukiah and leaving his wife and kid at home alone. I didn't know at the time that Larry and his wife were having problems of their own. Larry's dad grabbed me and pushed me down to the floor, trying to hit me, but I just blocked his punches. I didn't want to fight back out of respect, but when I'd had enough of his attacks, I hit him, knocking him into the refrigerator.

I went outside and took a long walk, trying to put things together in my head that I couldn't make any sense of. I was gone for about three hours before I finally went back to Larry's house. The front door was open, but no one was there.

I went into the bedroom and lay down on the bed, trying to get my heart to stop racing. I heard someone pull up outside, so I went to the door. It was Larry's older brother, who was also mad. This was just not my day. I should have stayed in Ukiah.

Well, I found Becky; she was over at a friend's house, crying on her shoulder. I asked Becky what was going on. This was her big excuse! "We were drinking, and I passed out. When I woke up you were standing at the door."

I said, "I guess you didn't know someone else was in the room with you. I guess you don't know anything about the hickey on the side of your neck either?"

After that day everything in my life started going south. Nothing was going good for me. We stayed together, trying to save what we had left of our marriage, which wasn't much. I guess I stayed with her because my daughter Kelli was my world. In time, I figured it would all pass, but I was wrong. Every time I closed my eyes, I could see it all over again. It was driving me out of my mind.

Chapter 29

Don't Shoot Me, I Work Here

Time went by, and I went to work as a security officer for the Naval Weapons Center. I was having a hard time holding down a good job. It seemed that every time I got one, I lost it or quit. On this job, we had to carry a firearm, but the problem was some of the people they hired had never used one before (smart, huh?). I was on patrol in the laboratory one night. One of the guards down at the other end of the hall had pulled back the hammer on his .357 and didn't know how to release it. He pointed it down the hallway, toward where I was just coming out of the door into the hallway. As I opened the door and started to step through it, I heard a *blam!*—he pulled the trigger. I waited for a few minutes and hollered to let him know I was down there. He had put his gun away by then. I asked him what in blazes was he thinking? He wasn't. That's when he told me what he did.

I looked at him and yelled, "You stupid idiot! You could have shot me or someone else!"

I took his gun away from him and went back to the command post. I told the sergeant what had happened. He said, "It was just an accident. Write a report on it."

Then he turned around and gave the guard his gun back. I told the sergeant he was just as stupid as the other guy as I walked out.

I was out of work for about a week when I heard about a job working at the Parsons Plant in Trona, California, as a gate guard. The people in charge there were good friends of mine, so I went right to work. It was an easy commute from where I lived in Ridgecrest.

Chapter 30

Snake Hunt

When I got off work, I would look for snakes on the road. It's just something I liked to do. I'd get a bunch of my friends to pile in my truck and go snake hunting at night. What you do is drive the back paved roads looking for rattlers at night because the snakes would crawl out on the road to get warm. When you'd see one, you'd stop and pick it up, play with it for a while, and then let it go. Not that easy! Snakes sense heat so when you bend down to pick them up, they will strike at you, and if you're not fast enough, you get bitten. We'd play chicken with them.

One night, we piled into my car, and I spotted a big snake along the side of the road, so I stopped and got out. When I approached it, I saw it was a Mohave Green. As I bent down to pick it up, I heard someone in the car scream. When they screamed, I jumped, and when I jumped the snake struck.

Before I could move out of the way, he bit my pant leg. I started jumping all over the place, trying to get that snake off my pants. Everyone in the car was laughing, saying I looked like I was doing a rain dance! I can imagine how I looked out in the middle of the street doing a chaotic dance. I didn't know at the time that a snake needs to snap its fangs into its prey. I finally got the snake off my pant leg. Before I could calm down, he'd slithered away into the desert. We would stay out all night until the sun started to come up. I was more than ready to go home that night!

One night, a friend and I were out in his VW bug looking for spots we could go to catch snakes. In truth, we hadn't intended to go snake hunting—we really just wanted to hang out and talk.

Suddenly I yelled, "Stop!"

Chris slammed on his brakes. I said, "I saw a snake lying beside the road—back up slowly."

Chris backed up his car and stopped. There on the side of the road was a four and a half foot Mojave Green rattler, one of the deadliest snakes in California. I had to catch it!

I got out of the car, and Chris pleaded, "Be careful! We are too far from any hospital, and if you get bitten, you'll die because I'm not sucking out the poison!"

A bite from a Mojave green rattler hits your nervous system, and you're dead within minutes if you don't get to a hospital. I finally caught the snake. Where could I put it for the ride home?

Chris had an empty bowling bag in his trunk, so I put the snake in there and shut the trunk. It was around 5:30 a.m. when we started back home. When we got to my house it was almost six thirty.

Chris pulled his car up in front of my house. "Hang on," I said. "I'll go get something to put the snake in."

I told Chris to get the bowling bag out of the car. When I came back out, Chris was standing at the front of his car with the bag in his hand. He had a strange look on his face. I asked him, "Chris, what's wrong?"

He stood there staring at me, looked down at the empty bag with a hole in it, and said, "Where's the snake?"

We started looking around the trunk and noticed there were two holes leading up to the inside of his car. I got inside the car and started hunting all over. No snake.

As I was getting out, I noticed a big lump in the headliner. "Chris, I found the snake!"

"Where?" Chris asked me.

"It's in the headliner inside the roof of the car over the driver's seat," he said.

"It's where? In the headliner of the car? That's just great!" Chris said. "How are we going to get it out?"

I replied, "I guess we could wait for it to die or leave the door open for a while and see if he gets thirsty and comes out on his own." Then I said, "I'll tell you what—I can undo the head liner just enough to get my hand in there and find where its head is and pull it out."

Chris looked at me and said, "Well, try not to rip my headliner."

"Oh, don't worry about me, Chris. I won't get bitten," I said sarcastically.

I slid my hand in and felt around. I could feel the rattles, so I followed the body until I found its head. I pulled it out very slowly and got him. He was huge! Chris told me afterward he wasn't going to get in that car until we got the snake out.

The next night, we decided to get some coffee after another big night of snake hunting. On the way home, a car pulled out in front of me and when I slammed on my brakes, the barrel I had in the back of the truck filled with snakes went flying—snakes and all! Here it is 3:30 a.m., and I'm out in the middle of the street in town picking up snakes. I'm just glad there weren't a whole lot of people out at that time of night. I got the snakes back in the barrel and got my coffee. What a wonderful world! Just when I thought we couldn't top this night, lo and behold—this next adventure was just plain freaky!

Chapter 31

Abducted or Not

One night around 11:00 p.m., my friend and drummer Boots and I were out riding motorcycles on the back roads out of town. It was one of those summer nights, about ninety-five degrees. On the way home, we stopped at the top of Trona Road overlooking Ridgecrest. This is going to sound weird, but it is the honest-to-God's truth.

We were sitting on our motorcycles talking about playing music. As we were talking, everything went deadly silent, and a bright light appeared overhead. Does this sound like a science fiction movie yet? Wait for it…

Let me start from the beginning. Before we went for our ride, Boots and I were at his house, talking about our ancestors. I was telling him about my great, great, great, grandfather, Benjamin Wade, who was one of the men conspiring to assassinate President Lincoln. Boots stared at me with his mouth wide open and said, "That's really strange because my great, great, great grandfather was John Wilkes Booth!" Then we decided to take a bike ride.

We laughed about our historical connection as we sat there on top of Trona Road—and then it happened. There wasn't a sound; not even the crickets were making any noise. Suddenly a bright light shone down on us. I looked up into the light, started to say something to Boots and that is the last thing I remembered. As God is my witness that's exactly what happened.

The next thing I remembered was sitting at the back of the 7/11 store downtown. I was in a daze. I got off my bike and walked around to the front of the store where I heard some people talking about a light in the sky. They said it went straight up and out of sight.

After that night, I started having blackout spells. I went to work for Parsons Company in Trona, California, where they were building a plant. I worked as a gate guard, doing my daily badge check around the plant. That meant I walk around to make sure the men were there and working. Every morning, they had to come through my gate, and I'd hand them their badges. Throughout the day, I would check on them. Some of them would check in, leave through one of the other gates and have their buddies turn in their badges. Anyway, I was up on the eighteenth floor doing my check and the next thing I remembered I was lying on the walkway. The men told me I was talking to some of the guys, I blacked out and almost went over the edge, when one of the guys grabbed me by my belt and pulled me back.

They sent me to a local hospital to get a checkup and on to Loma Linda Hospital for a complete checkup. I was there for a little over two weeks. They ran every test they could—I even had shock therapy—but they didn't find anything wrong. When I went back to work, I was called into the office. I was told they had to let me go because they couldn't risk that happing again. They apologized and said there was nothing else they could do.

I went home and started looking for work again. I decided to go out one night to one of the bars in town, a place called the Top Hat, and they hired me right on the spot. The band needed a lead singer, and they said I was the best for the job. I worked there for about a month when another club down the street contacted me and asked me to work for them. It made me feel good to know everyone wanted me to sing in their clubs. That is when I realized that being an entertainer was what I was meant to do. What happened next changed my life forever.

Chapter 32

Merle Haggard and JD's Club

One night, Jack Collier asked me if I would work with him. He asked me to play bass guitar and sing at JD's. This was the biggest club in town, not to mention the best band in town. Celebrities like Merle Haggard, Bonnie Owens, Billy Mize, and Tommy Cash always performed at JD's. Jack was the lead guitar player in the band.

The next night, as I started to get on the bandstand, the man running the card room came up to me and Jack. He told me I wasn't getting near the bandstand until I paid him what my father owed him. I told him I didn't have any idea what he was talking about. He said, "Either pay or leave."

Jack asked him how much my father owed him, and he answered, "Fifty dollars."

Jack said, "I'll pay you your money after work tonight."

The guy said, "Okay—have fun."

After that incident, I felt quite embarrassed, worried I couldn't do my job well. Jack told me, "Don't worry about it, it will be taken care of." Then he said jokingly, "I'll just take it out of your wages for the next five months."

The band consisted of Jack on lead guitar, Don McNatt on the drums, Jerry Ward on the bass guitar, and Norm Hamlet on steel guitar. I was the lead singer until I took over Jerry's job playing bass. We were together for about three years. The first time I met Merle Haggard was when he, Roy Nichols, and Don Markham came into JD's while I was playing bass guitar and doing the lead singing for my band. On break, Jack introduced us. Merle told me that he already knew about me—that Jack and Don had told him who I was. I believe he came in that night to see me perform, and later he took me aside and said, "They were right about you—I'm impressed."

I also worked in Bakersfield, about 145 miles away, with a lot of the country stars—Barbara Mandrell, Red Simpson, Joe and Rose Lee Maphis, and many more. That was one of the best times in my life.

I worked with Merle Haggard when he needed me or when his bass player, Bobbie Atkins, wanted some time off. One night during a break, Merle told Jack he wanted me to work with him and the Strangers as his new bass guitar player. Jack told me a few weeks later that Don McNatt told Merle I was too young and reminded Merle I had never been on the road before. He said I wouldn't last—it wouldn't be a very good idea. Jack and I talked with Hag and got things worked out so I could play bass for him when he was in town, which was a lot over the next six years.

Down the road, I started my own band called High Desert Drifters, and we opened at a new club at the other end of town called The High Desert Saloon. Eventually JDs went to rock and roll, so Jack and Don were out of work. I hired them to work with me. I wanted to go on the road for a while, but Jack and Don didn't want to go, so I put another band together.

My new band was called Shiloh. We opened at another club on the outskirts of town called Johnnie's Club. Johnnie's was traditionally a disco bar, but when Johnnie started losing his crowd, he decided to switch to country. He came to the High Desert Saloon and heard us play. He offered us a job at his club, which we took. We played at Johnnies until we were ready for the road.

Some of Bakersfield's country stars came out to do some shows, and boy, was the place packed! I started doing the booking for Johnnie's. I booked Bonnie Owens and her brother-in-law Mack Owens, who played steel guitar for Bonnie. I also booked Red Simpson and Joe and Rosie Maphis. I was drinking heavily at that time—everyone in the band was doing the same. We would sit around hours and talk and drink all night until the sun came up. One weekend, Lewis Talley and Merle came to the club, and we partied all night until the sun came up—then I went home to get some sleep. Even though I worked this way every night of the week, I was always there for my daughter and wife. The house we bought from Becky's mom was on two and one-half acres of land. I started clearing it so we could sell it.

During this time of my life, I had no idea what I was doing. I was always confused about my life, and I didn't know if I was coming or going most of the time. I always felt like I was from another planet. I was at the point where I didn't care if I lived or died. There would be times I would go off by myself just to think.

Ever since my youth, I have tried to deal with death. I remember when I was sixteen and working at a nursery watering the plants. I saw a man fall at the crosswalk and I ran out to see if he was all right. I lifted his head off the ground, put it on my lap and that's where he died—with me holding his head. When the police arrived, I told one of the officers the man was sleeping and that he'd told me he wasn't feeling very good. When the ambulance arrived, they put him on a stretcher and covered his head. That's when I knew the man had died.

I started doing stupid things like inviting my friends over to have séances at my houses. One night, a friend was complaining about his ex-girlfriend who wouldn't leave him alone. I told him just to tell her to flake off, but he said he couldn't because she wouldn't listen to him. I said, "Okay, let's try something. Let me try to hypnotize you and you can really tell her to get out of your life." He agreed to try it. I'd read about hypnoses but never actually tried it on anyone. I put Frankie under, told him that when he saw her, he wouldn't know who she was, he wouldn't like her, and if she didn't leave him alone, he would have her arrested for stalking. Then I woke him up and told him that he wouldn't remember any of this.

We all decided to go downtown and get some coffee at our favorite hangout. While we were there, guess who walked in? That's right, Frankie's ex-girlfriend. I said, "Let's see if it works!" I thought Frankie was faking it and wasn't truly under. She walked over to our table and asked Frankie if she could talk to him outside. Frankie ignored her at first, but she wouldn't give up. Frankie got up from the table, and I thought he was going to go with her. Instead, he laid into her like a raging bull. I looked at my friends in awe. As she stormed out the door, she said, "I don't know what's going on, but I'm going to call my father!"

Her father was a licensed psychiatrist and could get me into a whole lot of trouble. I said, "We have to get Frankie somewhere where I can reverse it!" Well, I did, and I told Frankie to tell her it was all a big joke. That was the last time I tried that again. And that was the last time I saw Frankie.

Jack was like a father to me. He got me my first job at JD's.

Where my mom and dad would go to
dance, Bakersfield, California

Chapter 33

The Hereafter

I still dabbled in the hereafter. I bought a new trailer and moved it downtown to a park. Becky's mother was babysitting our daughter Kelli one night, so we decided to have another séance in our trailer. We invited some friends over, turned out the lights and sat in a circle with candles. We had a Satanic Bible that we were reading from. In the back of the book, it explained how to call spirits from the other side. Well, we tried for about an hour and nothing happened. Everyone was getting tired and decided to call it a night, and Becky and I decided to go to bed.

About twenty minutes later, I heard something in the hallway. When I opened the bedroom door, did I get a big surprise! Standing in the hall was a figure of a human. I couldn't tell if it was a woman or man. All I know is it scared me! When I slammed the door and told Becky what I saw, she started screaming. Becky yelled, "Go get the book!"

That meant I had to go down the hallway, through the figure standing in the middle of the hallway, and on to the living room. I said, "I am not going out this door tonight!"

"You have to," she said, "because the book tells you how to send spirits back where they belong."

"No way!" I said, and we held each other and started praying out loud.

After a long time of prayer, I got enough courage to open the door again and look out. Picture this—me sneaking up to the door and opening it real slow to see if there's something there. If someone would have said anything or made a noise at that time, I probably would have had a massive heart attack! I opened the door and there was nothing there. I got the book, and it went directly into the trash can. After a couple of hours, we finally went to sleep. We never heard or saw anything like that again and I didn't fool around with the hereafter ever again.

Becky and I were always taking care of my nieces and nephew. We would gather them up and go across the street to the desert to catch snakes, but not the poisonous ones. I taught them what to look for and what not to pick up. Brian, my sister Martha's only son, was my favorite. They lived around the corner from us, and I took him everywhere I went. My other sister, Joyce, lived down at the other end of the park with her three girls, Kathy, Tammy, and Chrissie. We always had a houseful.

Chapter 34

Saved by an Angel

I loved to run around in the desert and up into the mountains by myself to think. One day, I decided to go mountain climbing in Red Rock Canyon, but this day I went with some friends of mine. I went off by myself and they took off in a different direction. While walking along a ledge, close to the top of one of the mountains, my foot slipped and down I went. I started sliding down the side of the slope because it was slippery shale. I tried to stop myself, but the shale was loose, and I kept sliding.

I looked down toward the bottom of the mountain and saw a mine shaft. I was sliding right up to the edge of it, unable to stop! As I approached the edge of the shaft, I came to a stop. My feet hung over the edge of the shaft. I was afraid to move because every time I tried to get up, I slid even closer to the edge. I tried to move some of the shale so I could use the hard rock underneath to stop myself, but I kept sliding closer until my knees hung over the edge. I was petrified and screamed for help, but I was too far away for anyone to hear me. I began praying intently to God to save my life.

As I lay on my back, I stretched out my arms, palms down, like a cross. I started moving my finger slowly, trying to reach that hard rock underneath the shale. I knew the shaft was deep because I couldn't hear the rocks hitting the bottom. There wasn't anyone for miles around, so yelling for help was futile. I knew I was going to die, and started feeling sick to my stomach. If I got sick, I would surely end up at the bottom of the shaft. I started thinking about my mom and what she would go through when she was told. I took a deep breath and started praying again. I don't think I had ever prayed as hard as I did that day. "Jesus, please help me now!"

In the next moment, my life changed forever! When I opened my eyes, I was lying back up on the top of the ledge, I'd slid down from. In front of me was the brightest, most wonderful light I had ever seen. In the middle of the light was a figure of a being, but I couldn't tell if it was male or female or even human. All I could see was the outline of a being in the light that resembled a cherub, sitting with its arms wrapped around its legs—head on knees—looking at me. I just kept staring. I felt a peace and calm I cannot explain. I turned my head to look down to the shaft where I had been a moment ago, and when I turned back around the figure in the light was gone—and I knew I was safe. I sat up and cried for what it seemed like hours. I know I saw a beautiful angel, sent by God to save my life that day.

When I finally met up with my friends, Rodney asked me where I had been. He said they were about to send a search and rescue out looking for me. He told me they were walking through the canyon hollering for me, and that I had been gone for nearly three hours. When I told them what happened, they started laughing and asked me if I found some pot while I was back there. It made me so angry I didn't say another word to them all the way home. After that day, I never spoke of my experience again. I know God sent an angel to save my life that day. I never did tell my mom, but she knows now after reading my book.

Chapter 35

Brookings, Oregon

My mother moved to Brookings, Oregon, with my stepfather. I told her Becky and I were having marital problems. She asked me if I wanted to come and visit for a while to clear my head and figure out what I wanted to do. She told me it might do us some good to be apart for a while, so we both could think. I talked to Becky, and she thought it would be a good idea. She sounded eager for me to leave. It was twelve-hour drive from my house to my mother's place in Oregon. That next morning, I left for my mom's, with no "Goodbye" or "I'll see you later." I arrived in Brookings around 10:00 p.m., called it a night and hit the sack. The next day my mom and stepfather took me on the grand tour around town. We made a trip to Crescent City as well to buy some Coors beer because you couldn't buy it in Oregon.

The next day after breakfast, I went looking for work. My first stop was the Eagles' Lodge in town. They asked me to come back that night and try out. I was glad a lot of people were there! They hired me to play every Friday and Saturday. I made $100 plus $50 to $100 in tips each night, so I was doing well for myself.

During the week, I went to a restaurant down the street for coffee around six o'clock. I'd sit in the back booth, away from people so I wouldn't bother them, and softly play my guitar and sing. One night, a waitress came over and said some of her customers wanted me to play a little louder so they could hear me. That started a new career for me! Every weeknight around dinner time I sat in that back booth, played, and sang. After a week quite a large crowd started gathering, requesting song after song. I was asked to move to one of the bigger booths because some of the younger crowd wanted to sit with me.

Wow, this was cool! We would have an old-fashioned singalong. I started making a lot of friends in and around Brookings. But I couldn't stop thinking about my wife back home.

After a week, I called home but there was no answer. I called my mother-in-law and she said, "Becky dropped Kelli off with me two nights ago."

I asked, "Where did she go?"

She replied, "I don't know. I haven't seen nor heard from her."

My mind started racing, and I began thinking of all kinds of scenarios. I went out to a bar that night and tried to drown my sorrows, but that didn't work.

I went to a friend's house because I needed to talk to someone. As I was getting ready to leave, I walked toward my car and the driver's door opened by itself. I looked at my friend and said, "I'm not getting in that car because I know I shut and locked the doors when I got here. That door was closed until I stepped off the porch."

I called my mother and asked if she would come and pick me up. She asked me about my car, and I said, "I'll tell you when you get here."

When she arrived, I told her what had happened, and she just stood there looking at my friend and me. He validated me, saying that what I told her was the honest-to-God's truth. I got into my mom's car, and she said we'd come back the next day to pick it up. As we drove away, I told her I wasn't about to get back in that car! I eventually picked it up a week later and drove it to my mom's house without a problem.

Things were back to normal until I called home again and my wife answered the phone. She sounded very strange. I asked her why she didn't answer the phone the last time I tried to call. She told me she went out with some of her friends. I asked her about our daughter, Kelli, and she told me she had a babysitter come over to watch her. "For two days?" I asked. "By the way, I spoke with your mother, and she told me Kelli was with her. She also told me she didn't know where you were." I asked her what was going on and she hung up on me.

I called a friend of mine who worked at one of the local bars, and he told me she was there just about every night drinking. I asked him if she was by herself, and he told me he didn't want to get in the middle of anything. I asked him again with a little more anger in my voice, and he finally told me she had been with some guy he had never seen before. I hung up without saying goodbye.

I was furious and sick at heart. I started pacing the room, wondering what I should do. My mom and stepfather were on the road driving truck. There wasn't anyone around to talk to, so I went down to the closest bar. After drinking for who knows how long, I decided to take a drive out of town. The further I drove the angrier I got. I stopped by the side of the road and got sick. I sat there for a while until I decided life wasn't worth it. I just wanted to end it all, but I had no idea what I wanted to do. I started driving again and headed for the bridge out of town. I aimed the car at the bridge and closed my eyes. The next thing I knew, I was sitting in my car with the rear end facing the bridge.

I had blacked out and when I awoke, I was completely confused. I sat there crying until the sun came up. I drove back to my mothers. When my mom came home, I didn't tell her what happened. I decided to get a divorce and go my own way.

When I asked myself how the car got turned around, I realized God had intervened on my behalf again.

Chapter 36

Music in Coos Bay

The next day, I called the agent in Coos Bay and set up a time to meet. I drove there the very next day and met with Leroy at his house. I told him I would love to work with him. He said I could stay it his house for the night until we could make other arrangements.

In the morning, he called the other band members to get together for some rehearsal. Leroy's wife was very nice; she said I could stay in the spare bedroom until I could find my own place.

That next day, we all got together at the Balboa Club outside Coos Bay. I didn't know it at the time, but Leroy was the bass player for the band and Pete Oden was the leader. Pete played lead guitar and did most of the singing. He was a lot older than the rest of us.

My first mistake was getting on the bandstand. My second was showing them I could play bass—problem was that I played it better than Leroy. The third mistake was opening my mouth to sing. When I started singing, I could feel the heat coming from behind me where Pete was standing.

After I finished singing the band took a short break, and everyone went to a table at the back of the room. I followed and when I started to sit down, Pete asked me to wait over by the bandstand. So wait I did.

I noticed that the bartender joined them. The club was closed during the day, so that's when the band would practice. I heard Pete say with a very loud voice "We don't need another singer and we already have a bass player." I knew he did not want me to hear that.

My first band in Coos Bay Oregon. (Left to right) Roger Wade, Steve, Dale Roberts, and Pete Oden (center in black)

Pete got up from the table and left the club. Leroy came over to where I was sitting and said the club owner wanted to meet me, so we went to the bar where he was standing. He shook my hand and said, "I haven't heard anyone sing like that in I don't know how long."

I thanked him and he said, "Don't thank me. You're going to bring in a lot of money and people."

I looked at Leroy and asked him what was going on. He told me I was the new bass player.

I said "No, I can't take your job."

Leroy said, "I'm just filling in until they could find someone to take the job, and you fit the bill perfectly."

"What about Pete?" I asked.

"You will eventually take his place as lead singer," Leroy answered. *Wow*, I thought, *Pete's not going to like that.*

Leroy introduced me to the guys in the band and they all were great. They told me, "It's about time we got someone in here who can sing."

The members of the band were some of the best musicians in town: David Kipper on drums, Dale Roberts on steel guitar and Pete Oden, lead guitar and lead singer. For the first couple of weeks, Pete would let me sing only three or four songs a night. Every time we took a break people came up to me and ask why I wasn't singing much. I told them they would have to ask the owner, so they did. A couple nights later, I became the lead singer in the band. We had a pretty good band.

The club was packed every night and the club owner was happy. We performed there for two years. The band and I had gotten tired of Pete's attitude, so we spoke with the club owner and told him we were leaving because of it. He said, "Oh no, you're not! Roger is the main reason everyone comes here. Let me talk to Pete and I'll call you."

That next Thursday, he called and said, "I fired Pete and the club is all yours." We stayed there for three more years until the club burned down. Although we had most of our things out, David lost his drums, and I lost my amplifier. The club did replace them.

Chapter 37

Back to Ridgecrest

After that, I decided to go back to Ridgecrest to see my daughter. Becky and I thought we'd try to see if we could put things back together again, so I gave it one more try.

One day, while I was home with Kelli, Becky said, "I'm going to the store. I'll be back in a few minutes." After she left, I went into the kitchen to fix something for us to eat.

Suddenly, Kelli started chocking. I rushed into the living room and found her lying on the floor. Next to her was an orange juice bottle Becky was using for her turpentine. She was working on a paint-by-number picture and left the bottle on the table. Kelli thought it was orange juice and drank it. I grabbed Kelli and smelled her breath—it smelled of turpentine. I put her on the kitchen table and started pouring milk down her as fast as she could drink. I grabbed her and ran over to the neighbor's house, yelling, "Take me to the emergency room! Kelli can't breathe!"

We jumped in the car, and within a couple of minutes, we were there. Luckily, the hospital was just around the corner. They rushed Kelli in and put her in an oxygen tent. I tried to call Becky, but she didn't answer her phone. Next,

I called her mother, explained to her what had happened, and I said, "Tell Becky where we are if she calls you."

Becky arrived the hospital about three hours later. I was so worried about Kelli, I didn't even ask her where she was and I really didn't care. I stayed with Kelli all the time she was in the hospital—I didn't want to leave her side.

The second night, Kelli almost died from pneumonia. A few days later, we got to take her home. I stayed with Kelli until she was fully recovered.

Becky and I moved to the new Wherry Housing track where I started a landscaping business. I kept the business for about a year until it made enough money to take care of itself. I had a great crew, so all Becky had to do was make out their checks at the end of the week.

I went out on the road with my band again, and when I returned home, Becky told me she was pregnant again—this time, with my son Sean.

Around Sean's first birthday, we had trouble in our marriage again, and it was worse than ever. I told Becky I was leaving for good this time. We decided it would be the best decision for both of us if I went my own way and she went hers.

I went back to work at Johnnie's Club five nights a week, but things weren't the same. I asked the guys if they were ready to hit the road and they all said jokingly, "We're not gone yet?"

We all decided to head out of town to start a new adventure. Our first gig was in Bishop, California, at the bowling alley. That's where I met my second wife, Patty.

Chapter 38

Sorry, My Mistake

While working at the bowling alley, I became good friends with George, the bouncer. One night while on a break, he said, "I want you to meet my sister!"

I laughed and told him, "You don't even have a sister!"

He replied, "Yes, I do! She's over there at that table."

He walked me over to a table where four young women were sitting and said, "Roger, this is my sister Patty. Patty, this is Roger."

Patty said, "I know who he is—he's the singer in the band."

When the gig was over, I went back home and told Becky that I wanted a divorce. I was going back on the road for quite a long time. The band was ready to go, so the next day we were on the road again. This time, we headed to the King Falls Lounge in Klamath Falls Oregon. Patty and her brother went with us. George helped set up and tear down every night. I put the band together and was doing all the bookings.

The first week at the club Mike, the drummer, met a girl who was the dealer where he was playing cards. They started going out and were together the entire time we worked there. Mike came to me and said they wanted to get married in the club. I thought it was a great idea. They were married right on the bandstand the following night while we were on break. The next day, Patty and her brother headed back home. She and I were not getting along.

Our next stop was Boise, Idaho. While in Boise, I decided to go out by myself to another club. I wanted to check out the other bands in town. I finally got up enough nerve to ask a young lady to dance, and afterward, I walked her back to her table. She asked me if I wanted to join her and her girlfriend, which I did. We enjoyed a great night of dancing and talking about the bands around town. It was fun not performing for one night and just hanging out.

On our way to the band's next gig, Patty called and asked if she could come back. I said she could, long as there weren't any more problems. I picked her up at the bus station on the way to our next stop in Walla-Walla, Washington, and the Lamplighter Club.

After a gig at the Lamplighter, we headed to Canada to play at the Shooters Club in Regina, Saskatchewan. Our band Shiloh had become a big hit in Canada. While we were at the Shooters Club, they hired a mobile recording studio to come in and do a full album, which we thought was great. People gave us the nickname "Little Alabama" because we sounded so much like the band "Alabama."

After leaving Saskatchewan, we went to Medicine Hat, Alberta. The hotel we stayed at was old and creepy, and one night after work, we decided to go exploring. The hotel was about eight stories high and the top three floors were unoccupied, so up we went—Mike and his wife Debbie, Patty, and me. On the way up, I told everyone about the murders

I'd heard about that had happened upstairs. Debbie held on to Mike like glue. I opened one door to a room with a broken window, which the wind was blowing through and making weird noises. When we walked in the room the door slammed shut behind Debbie, who let out a scream. We all laughed so hard, I was crying. Debbie said she wasn't going down without the rest of us. I found an old doctor's bag that had a letter in it written to a lady in the 1800s—cool!

We hooked up with an agency called the Paul Edgerton Agency. We were at rehearsal one day when Paul introduced a young girl to us. He wanted to know if she could travel with us as a guest star in our shows. Since he was our booking agent, I couldn't say no. I gathered the band together and asked what they thought. They said if we were going to get paid more money it was okay with them. I agreed.

I went to my room to tell Patty what was going on so she wouldn't wonder who the girl was. She immediately got angry and started yelling. This time I sent her to my mother's place in Coos Bay, Oregon.

Our next stop was Edmonton, Alberta, and then on to Kamloops, British Columba. From there, we went to White Horse in the Yukon. After playing a month there, we went on to Weyburn, Saskatchewan, almost right back to where we started. This is where some of the band members decided they wanted to snort cocaine. I just happened to walk in right in the middle of it. "You guys know what the rules are about drugs in the band," I said. "If you get busted, we all go down for it."

Donnie said, "We're not going to get busted!"

I said, "You just did, and I'm sorry to say it but you're both fired."

One of the guys said, "You can't fire us! You won't have anyone to finish the gigs."

I told him to let me worry about that, and I left. I went to my room and called the Musicians Union in Los Angeles. They had a drummer and a guitar player up the next day before we had to go to work. I was down in the club when the two guys I fired came walking in. Mike said, "See? I told you that you needed us to finish the gig."

Just about that time, the two new musicians who were replacing them walked in, and I introduced them. They just sat there with their mouths open, then got up and left. They were both gone by the time the gig was over. I didn't see them again until I went back Idaho to pick up some things that I'd left there. Neither of them was mad at me because they knew they had broken the by-laws we all signed. They were working in a club across the state line in Ontario, Oregon, and asked me if I would work with them again because neither were good singers. I hired them back again and gave them a second chance.

Patty was still living with my mother while I was on the road performing. A girl I met in Boise showed up one night with some of her friends. While it was good to see her again, Patty and I had gotten back together. We moved to Hermiston, Oregon, where we both worked for Simplot Company. We worked there for six months, and it was a great job.

While we were there, I got back into martial arts. I started practicing daily, and I worked on my car the rest of the time. I bought a 1969 El Camino with an automatic that I converted to four on the floor. I painted it gunmetal gray and placed chrome rims on it.

When Simplot shut down, Patty and I moved to Payette Idaho. Patty got a job as a dispatcher for the Payette County Sheriff's Department. I went to work at the club across the border in Ontario, Oregon, playing music with my old band members. After falling out with them again, I quit and went to work at the sheriff's department where Patty was employed. What unfolded at that job made me realize I am better off having a job as an entertainer—it's a job that's much safer too!

Chapter 39

Sheriff's Department

I was hired at the sheriff's department as a reserve officer at first, and then I went full time. Mom came down to live with us, which was great until my girlfriend, Patty, threw one of her tantrums and told my mom to go live with my sister. At that point I was ready to tell her to take a hike for good. My mom chose to move back in with my sister, even though I didn't want her to. I wish I could have seen what was in my near future.

I was having a lot of trouble with my health at that time, so I wasn't in the mood to fight with my girlfriend. While she worked at the sheriff's office, I was home by myself. One day, suddenly, I couldn't breathe. I had pain in my chest that felt like a heart attack. I tried to reach the phone to call the sheriff's office, but only got halfway to it before I collapsed on the floor. I crawled to the phone, called 911, and blacked out before I could speak with anyone. They traced the call and were there in minutes. They rushed me to the hospital and told me I'd had a stress attack. Living with my girlfriend, I could see why. It's a wonder it wasn't a heart attack—but then again maybe it was, and I didn't know it.

Soon after I returned to work, we got a call about gun-shots heard coming from one of the two story houses on the outskirts of town. When we arrived, we checked the perimeter of the house and found no one around. We then checked the inside of the house. My sergeant told me to check the rooms upstairs while they checked the bottom floor. That was the longest stairway I ever walked up. It was scary not knowing what was waiting for me at the top of those stairs.

When I got to the top, I found a man sitting at the foot of a bed with an AK47 tucked under his chin. It looked like he was trying to pull the trigger but couldn't reach it with his finger. I called my sergeant and stayed with the man and waited.

My sergeant told me to go check the other two rooms, so I did. The first room was empty, but the second one I found two girls, aged ten and sixteen. Both girls had been shot once in the head, both were dead. We found out later the sixteen-year-old was pregnant. After seeing them, I wanted to take him out myself. I will never forget that day for as long as I live.

I wanted to make a difference in the world, but I wasn't sure this line of work was it.

Chapter 40

Police Department

A couple of weeks later, I went to work for the New Plymouth Police Department, which was about ten miles from Payette. New Plymouth is located out in the country in the ranch lands. I was on patrol and out of my vehicle when a man driving an old gray Buick sped by. I recognized him as someone I'd arrested may times before. I jumped in my car and began pursuit. The car was headed for the freeway, which was twenty-two miles from town. I couldn't let that car get to the freeway or I would lose it. Putting pedal to the medal, I was just about to catch up when the car I was pursuing's tail lights went out. Fortunately, there was a full moon out, enabling me to see a long way without my lights on. Not seeing any cars on the long road ahead I slowed down, looking off to the side of the road.

I came up to a dirt road next to the canal. There I saw the headlights of a car upside down in the bottom of the canal. I pulled onto the dirt road, called for backup, and jumped out of my patrol car. I looked around to see if he had jumped out of the car before it went into the canal. As I was about to jump into the canal, the driver of the car came swimming up to the bank. I called out, "Are you okay? Is there anyone else in the car?"

He answered no and said, "Can you help me?"

I helped him out, put the handcuffs on him and got him into the back of my patrol car. It was then that the deputy finally showed up.

There were lots of things happening in this little town. Patty still worked for the sheriff's department, dispatching for the small towns around the county. While at work one night a deputy sexually harassed her. She called her lieutenant at home, and he just laughed at her. I was working the fair when a call came over my radio. It was my girlfriend, Patty, who told me to call her on the land line.

"What's up?" I asked.

She proceeded to tell me what happened. I told her to write a report and not to leave anything out. We were both beginning to have serious doubts about our employment.

There was a bright side during this period in my life. On my days off, I spent time helping kids in town. Sometimes I would be the go-between for them and their parents. If they had a personal problem, they would call me to talk. The kids nicknamed me Cop Roger and I was beginning to feel like I could make a positive difference in the community. However, as things began to get strange, I knew it was not meant to be.

I was on patrol one night on the outskirts of town, alone, and I noticed a man in a vehicle driving erratically. I turned on my overhead lights and pulled the car over. When I approached the vehicle, it smelled strongly of alcohol. I ask the driver to step out of the car and put his hands on top of it. I wanted to make sure he had no weapons on him.

I did a sobriety test, and he kept saying, "Apparently you don't know who I am."

I said "Apparently, yes I do know who you are, and you were driving under the influence."

"So," he said, "are you going to take me home?"

I replied, "If you call jail your home, then yes."

About that time, my chief pulled up and looked into the back of my patrol car. "Roger, do you know—"

I stopped him short and replied, "Yes, I know, it's the mayor. So what? He was breaking the law, and now he is going to jail. Any questions?"

I proceeded to get into my patrol car and drove the mayor directly to the jail.

There was another incident that was troubling to me. We were on a domestic dispute call and had made an arrest. The detainee was handcuffed and shouting incessantly in the back seat. My partner got out of the police car, opened the back door, and became physical. I witnessed my partner using excessive force, choking the detainee. I got out, pulled my partner off him, and told him to get back in the front seat, which he did. When we returned to the police station, I wrote up my report stating exactly what happened.

I noticed a coldness in the police department after that day, one that I could not shake or dismiss. I would soon find out that my intuition was unfortunately correct, and that something was terribly wrong.

After these encounters, I would make a stop, and no one would show up to back me up. I would go into a bar fight alone, call for backup and no backup would come. One day, I pulled over a stolen car with four men in it. I called for backup, and when no one came, I had dispatch call my chief since he lived close to where I was. At least he showed up, but it was after I had handled this dangerous situation on my own—which never should have happened. It put my life at risk, and that was extremely unsettling. These things began to bother me more and more. I didn't feel safe out there, and I felt alone.

One day, I found out someone was spreading rumors that I was doing rituals with the kids in town. I told my chief, "That's it. I've had enough! I am resigning." That was the last straw that broke this camel's back. I gave him my notice.

Payette County Sheriff's Department

Roger L Wade

Sherriff's Department

New Plymouth Police Department

Chapter 41

Number 1 KUZZ Radio

The next day, we packed our things and moved back to Coos Bay. I went to work at a club in North Bend playing music and getting drunk. I guess I was trying to drink my memories away, but it didn't help—it just made everything worse.

I sold all my equipment, we moved to Bakersfield, and I started working for security and bodyguard company. I began doing things that people just don't normally do. I was taking high-risk jobs other officers wouldn't take. You might think I was a little suicidal, and you would be right! I didn't care too much either way if I lived or died at this point in my life, so taking huge and dangerous risks was not that big a deal. I started serving subpoenas, worked part time in the mental ward at the hospital, and worked part time repossessing cars.

One night, Patty and I decided to go out and stopped in a small bar in Oildale, California. While we were there, I asked the band if I could sing a few songs with them—which I did. After I got off the bandstand, I was approached by a woman who owned the bar. She was in the back room where a card game was in process when she heard me singing. She asked me if I had any tapes with me and I handed her one of my demo cassettes. She stuck it in her player and played the first song. Before the song was finished, she turned it off, walked over to another man sitting at the card table, spoke to him, and then turned to me and said, "Can I buy you lunch?"

I said, "I guess so."

I soon discovered that she wanted to be my personal manager. I talked to my girlfriend about the offer, and we both agreed it would be a good idea.

My new manager said I needed to put a band together so she could get us booked. I started making some phone calls to my musician friends around Bakersfield. I found a lead guitar player, a drummer, steel player, and harmonica player. With me playing bass, I ended up with a five-piece band. We were all professionals, so it didn't take long for us to get it together as a band. My manager started getting us bookings all around Bakersfield.

Everywhere we played people wanted our records. We even went to Lion's Studio somewhere around Newport Beach. We recorded there for three days. When we were done, the recordings were sent to Capital Records in Hollywood for mastering. About a month later we received eight cases of 45 records. On side A was a song I wrote "The Devils Loss" and side B was a song Marty Robbins recorded called "You Gave Me a Mountain." My manager took my record to Bakersfield radio station KUZZ Radio for some airtime. The first week the song "The Devils Loss" was out it went from number 14 to number 1 on the charts. I was driving down the freeway in Bakersfield when

I first heard my song over the radio. What a shock to hear yourself on the radio!

We bought a Golden Eagle Greyhound bus so we could go out to promote our new record. I spent over a month inside fixing it up, gutting it first, then rebuilding it so we could live in it while we were on the road. Soon, my manager ruined everything by telling me she my girlfriend had to stay home so I could be seen with other women for publicity purposes.

I told her, "I'm not leaving her at home while I'm out running around the countryside with other women."

My manager then told me, "I'm going to keep all of your records and the money made from them and take the bus back if you don't do what I say."

"Sorry," I told her. "It's not going to happen."

Bakersfield Country

Just another show

My Bakersfield Band

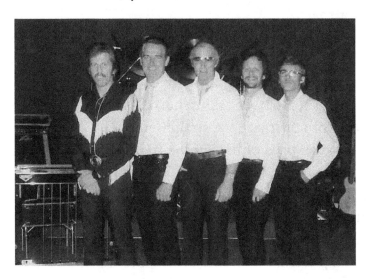

Chapter 42

Reno, Nevada

Before we moved, I entered the Wrangler Talent contest. Again, someone in charge didn't like the rules so they made up their own. I guess if you have money, you can do whatever you wish. After the contest was over, a judge I knew told me the contest was rigged. We got a standing ovation after our song. A teenage girl who performed a dance routine won instead. We were told her father paid to get her that win.

After everything fell apart, Patty and I packed up and moved to Reno. I was so mad! Here we go again—everything I worked so hard for—gone again. Before we headed to Reno, I remember asking her, "When will it ever stop? When will our music life straighten out?"

I was so tired of having the rug pulled out from under me repeatedly.

When we got to Reno, we parked our van outside her aunt's house, and that's where we stayed for two weeks. I was up and out every day looking for work and finally found a job singing in one of the local bars. That's when I started drinking again and getting into fights. After several altercations at the bar, I quit and applied for a security position at the Comstock Casino. I was hired that same day.

As the days went by, the job got even better. We would have calls to break up fights in the bar as well as stopping people trying to steal money.

One day, I walked by the dice table, and there on the floor was a fifty-dollar bill. I picked it up and asked if anyone at the table had dropped any money. The guy at the end of the table said, "I must have dropped it." I asked him what it was. He looked down at the money he had in his hand and said, "It was a fifty-dollar bill." I jokingly asked him what the date was and started laughing. He glared at me as I handed him his money. He said, "I guess you thought you were going to keep it."

"No," I said as I turned and walked away. "I would have turned it in."

I went back to making my rounds around the casino, and every time I passed by the dice table the guy made a sarcastic remark to me. After three more rounds of those remarks, I called my supervisor and reported what was happening. He told me to escort him out the door. That's all I wanted to hear. I called my partner and told him I had to take the trash out. He said, "I'll be right there!" I walked up to the table and tapped the gentleman on the shoulder, told the dealer to cash him out, that the gentleman was leaving.

"Don't know who I am?" he stated.

I replied, "I really don't care who you are. You are leaving."

He asked me, "On what grounds?"

I told him, "Oh, I could say I just don't like you and I especially don't like your smart mouth. You are leaving now. You can walk out like a gentleman, or we can drag you out."

I told him if he didn't leave the casino, I was going to throw him out. Then all hell broke loose. He started to walk out of the casino and then turned and took a swing at us. I don't know which one of us hit him first—me or my partner—but down he went. I put the handcuffs on him and called the police to come and pick him up. When the police officer got there, he said, "Do you know who that is?"

I said, "Yes, the idiot that got himself thrown in jail."

The officer said he was a prize fighter here in Reno to fight. I just laughed and said, "Well, he got his fight, didn't he?"

Patty and I decided to get married during our time in Reno. We took Shotokan Karate together. One day at practice I was sparring with one of the black belts. It was supposed to be non-contact. He tried to kick me in the side and when I blocked his kick, and without putting his foot down, he came over my shoulder and kicked me right in the mouth. When he saw how mad and bloody I was, he started backing up as fast as he could to get away from me. The sensei stepped in and stopped the fight. He said he was just testing me to see how I would handle myself. I was so mad. I told Patty, "I'm done. This place is a joke," and walked out.

For a long time, I tried to think of a way to get even with him, so I joined the Coalition of Martial Artists, hoping I'd be able to fight him again. It didn't happen, but I took my anger out on everyone else on the mat.

I started teaching self-defense classes to the security personal around Reno. One of my students was a security officers at the Comstock Casino. He was one of my best friends. He didn't have a place to stay, so Patty and I told him he could stay with us until he could find a place of his own. Patty and I had just gotten off work, cashed her payroll check, and gone home. Robbie came in a little bit later, and we sat and talked for a while. It was getting late so we said our good nights and hit the sack. The next morning when we awoke, Robbie was already up and gone. So was the money from Patty's paycheck she'd cashed the night before, along with a $600 coat I'd bought in Canada. I called The Comstock and learned he'd gone to work and stolen one of the cash boxes. I was asked to come down to talk to the police. I went outside and guess what? He'd stolen my car I had just bought three weeks earlier. I tracked down my car to a used car lot in Carson City where he'd sold it. How he sold it to them without the right paperwork, I don't know. I did get my car back and Robbie was busted four states over.

This was the car Robbie stole.

This is what it looked like after I got it back and fixed it up.

Chapter 43

The Ranch

We moved back to Coos Bay and opened a karaoke business in a Chinese restaurant in North Bend. We traveled up and down the coast selling karaoke machines. At the time, no one knew what karaoke was, so we had to demonstrate every place we went to. We were approached by people who owned a furniture store in North Bend, Oregon. They wanted us to open a recording studio in the back room, so we did. I started building a karaoke juke box to make my business better. After I finished it, the owner of the store decided to call a company in Los Angeles and sell it to them. The next thing I know, three men were standing in my studio asking questions about my system. About six months later, they came out with a karaoke juke box. That's what can happen when you don't get a copyright before you show your invention to others.

The next part of my story is strange. While Patty and I sold karaoke machines at a fair in Eugene, Oregon, I felt it was time to pack up and head for home. We agreed, so we started breaking everything down. As we were walking out of the building, I noticed two people I'd gone to school with from my hometown of Ridgecrest, California. As I took a few more steps, I realized who they were. They were standing there holding hands, looking at me and smiling. As I approached them, a group of people came out of the building they were standing in front of, making it difficult for me to see them. When I got to where they had been standing, they were gone. It was like they were never there. I know what I saw, and no one will ever convince me I didn't. Here's their story.

I will call the boy Roy and the girl Deb. Roy loved to race cars. He had one of the fastest cars in town. One night, Roy and Deb were coming home from a night out and Roy was going too fast around a curve. He lost control of the car, it rolled, and they were both killed instantly. The two people I had just seen in this present moment were the two who died in that car accident back in my high school days.

I sat down next to the fountain in the middle of the square trying to figure out what just happened. Patty asked me, "What's wrong? You look like you've just seen a ghost!"

I said, "How about two of them?" After I told her what had just happened, she looked as if she'd seen a ghost as well!

Right about that time, a woman ran up to us and said, "I was trying to catch you before you left. I'm glad you stopped."

That's where we first met Bonnie. Bonnie was from Cloverdale, California, and she wanted us to help her get a karaoke business started where she lived. I couldn't get what happened off my mind, so I told Bonnie about what had just happened to me. She told me they were keeping me there to meet her!

We went back to Cloverdale where Bonnie and Dan lived. Dan was managing an eighteen-thousand-acre cattle ranch at the time and they said we could stay in their spare bedroom. It was neat because I would go with Dan every morning and help him with the ranch chores. There were two parts to the ranch: one half was the area Dan and Bonnie lived—the other six thousand acres was on the other side of the mountain with a house on it.

After a couple of weeks went by, Dan asked me if we'd like to take care of the other side of the mountain. He told me he could give me $1,000 a month plus the house. "Can we go over and look at it?" I asked.

We jumped in the jeep and over the mountain we went. All the roads were dirt, so you had to have a four-wheel drive vehicle to get around the ranch. Lucky for me, they let me use one of their four-wheel drive trucks.

Everything seemed to be working out just fine. Patty and I moved in, and I started working for Dan (or shall I say, I started doing his job and mine). He had me building culverts and fences and feeding the cattle. After grading the roads, we would occasionally help Bonnie with her karaoke business. Everything was going well. Patty and I were at Dan and Bonnie's for dinner, having usual dinner conversation. Bonnie said something to Patty, which I guess Patty didn't like. She lit into Bonnie, got up, and walked out of the house. Patty was the kind who could never hold her temper or her tongue. That was the last time they spoke to each other.

Soon after that evening, everything went south. I was doing all the work, like feeding the cows up in the mountains, cleaning out the stalls and mending fences. I was carrying railroad ties, barbed wire, fence posts, and the post pounder up and down hills and carrying railroad ties by myself.

One day, Dan sent me to the back forty to cut some trees for firewood. I was cutting a limb, and suddenly, another limb switched back and rolled on me, crushing my left arm. I couldn't move because the limb was too big and heavy. I had to dig around my arm until I could pull it out. I finally was able to slide my arm free, but now I couldn't move it. I called Dan, but there was no answer.

I finally made my way to the truck, only to find I had another problem. I was driving a four-wheel drive truck with a stick shift. I had to shift gears with my right hand and drive the truck with it as well. I had one hell of a time getting down the mountain. Halfway down, I started getting the feeling back in my left arm, which meant the pain started coming. When I got to the main house Dan was sitting on the porch. "So are you done cutting the wood?" he asked. He didn't even ask me what happened to my arm, which was bloody by now.

I asked him if he could take me to the doctor's office. He answered, "You have a car. I can't leave the ranch. Your arm doesn't look that bad, just some scratches."

I got in my car and left. My left arm was crushed from my elbow down to my wrist. The doctor bandaged me up and put my arm in a sling. He told me I'd be out of work for at least six months to a year. No lifting, pushing, or using my arm at all for a while. I went back and gave Dan the note the doctor had given me. Dan told me to go home and rest, which I did.

The next day, I received a phone call from Dan. He said, "The owner of the ranch wants you to speak with you."

I hung up and went to the office, where the owner, Hale, and Dan were waiting for me. The owner said, "Dan tells me you haven't been doing your work around here. Is that true?"

I replied, "No way! I've been doing mine and his too."

"That's not what I hear. What happened to your arm?" Hale asked.

When I told him what happened, Hale said, "If you can't work, you'll have move off the ranch."

"I haven't anywhere to go at this time," I responded.

"I'll give you a couple of weeks to find somewhere to live."

I just glared at Dan, not believing he just stood there and let this happen. When I told Patty what had just happened, she was so mad she wanted to go have a little talk with Mr. Hale. I told her, "Don't waste your breath."

The next day, we left for her mother's house in southern California. She gave us a small trailer, which I hooked up, and away we went back to Cloverdale. We parked it at the KOA campgrounds and put everything we had in storage. Thank God Kevin and Johnnie, our friends in Cloverdale, helped us move everything in one day.

I filed for workmen's comp and received compensation for my injury, but it was nothing compared to almost losing my arm. I wanted to sue Hale, but I couldn't find a lawyer who would take my case. Old man Hale was a millionaire and everyone I spoke with told me he could hang on for years, and I'd end up with nothing for my troubles.

Our ranch house

Mom and I on the porch

Just a day's work on the ranch

Roger Wade

Chapter 44

Moving Off the Ranch

I went to work at the KOA after my arm healed a little. On the weekends, I played music for the guests. I started building fireplaces for each campsite, which lasted a few months. Next, we began playing music at the American Legion Hall in town, so that's where we moved our trailer. We had a lot of fun playing there.

We went over to Kevin and Johnnie's during the week for Bible studies. Sometimes I took my keyboard over for sing-alongs—we had some great times.

One day, I decided to call an old school buddy I hadn't seen for years. He was living in Granite Bay, California, and he decided to come up to see me. He made a lot of money selling real estate in California. He invited us to stay with him for a week, so I took him up on his offer. While there, we talked about buying a condo in Roseville, California. Since he owned a property there, he said he would carry the paperwork of us. We took the trailer back to my wife's mom and moved into the condo.

Things were going great. I went to work for a small mailing business in Roseville until I stated getting performance bookings for us out of town. For next year, we'd go to Wendover, Nevada, for two weeks, and then Elko for two weeks. Just as things were getting good, it happened. The owner of our condo asked Patty if she'd watch his two girls while he was at work. I told her that I had a bad feeling and didn't think it was a very good idea. She did it anyway. Two days later, while Patty was in the kitchen, the girls' stepmother came by to pick them up. She left without telling Patty. Their father, one of my best friends, was mad at Patty, but it wasn't really her fault. After that, Patty decided she didn't want to buy the condo. I had to make a hard decision—either go against Patty and lose her, or take Patty's side, and lose one of my best friends from high school. I decided to stay with my wife. I believed in my wedding vows, for better or for worse.

Chapter 45

On the Road Again

We got booked in Arkansas, and we had a week to get there. On the way, my wife picked up a case of strep throat, so I took her to the hospital in Oklahoma City. They gave her a shot and sent us on our way. In Dallas, Texas, at my sister Joyce's, I found Patty lying on the floor in the bathroom so I rushed her to the hospital. Getting to the hospital wasn't easy. A tornado hit earlier that evening and when we left, rain was coming down so hard, I couldn't see the road. Once we arrived at the hospital, we waited for over an hour. Patty was getting worse, and I was getting angry. I told the receptionist if she didn't get some help right away, I was going to tear the place apart, starting with her office. She immediately got on the phone, and someone arrived with a gurney. They took us back to one of the rooms and started an IV on Patty. After an hour, she started feeling better.

I took her to my sisters for the night, and the next morning, she was feeling okay, so we left for Arkansas. We spent a few weeks there, headed back to Wendover, Nevada, for my fiftieth birthday, and then to Elko, Nevada, for another two weeks.

Stopped in Nashville. I had to see Elvis.

This was our transportation.

Chapter 46

The Big Change

We finished setting up our equipment and settled into our room. We received an invitation from our entertainment director to go across the street to another casino. At the time, I didn't know he had his own agenda, but we were there to listen to the band and do some dancing. I went to the restroom, and when I returned, I couldn't find my wife or the entertainment director. I asked around and found out they had gone downstairs where they kept old tables and chairs. I went to the door to go down, but the door was locked, and she wouldn't answer her phone. When they came back up, I asked her what they were doing. She told me he was showing her the room where they kept all the old tables.

Next, she said, "Let's go in where the band is playing."

When we sat down the entertainment director asked me if he could dance with my wife. I replied, "You'll have to ask her."

They got up and danced, and when Patty came back to the table she told me, "I am going to sit at the bar—I have some thinking to do."

When I told Patty I was going back to the room, she said she would be there in a few minutes. I became worried after thirty minutes had gone by and Patty had not returned.

I went back to the casino and found my way to the bar. I saw the entertainment director there with my wife standing between his legs. I walk up to them and said, "What's going on here?"

Patty retorted, "I told you I wanted to be alone."

I replied, "This sure doesn't look to me like you're alone."

The guy she was with started to get up and say something. I glared at him and said, "You'll be a walking dead man." He slid back down in his chair.

I told Patty, "Go back to our room—I will be right behind you."

Instead of causing a scene, I turned and walked out of the casino. Patty wasn't too far behind me. I went into our room and said, "Okay, what's going on, Patty?"

She looked at me and simply said, "I don't want to be married anymore."

I stared at her in disbelief and said, "You are going to throw our marriage away over some scrawny little jerk?"

She answered, "I'm going to get my own room, and as of this moment, we are separated."

I stood there feeling numb and stunned. I asked her, "What about our job? We still have one full week of shows to perform."

She replied, "Don't worry, I'll do my job."

I called my mother because she was also my best friend. I relayed what had just happened.

She said, "You've got to be kidding me."

"I don't know what to do," I said.

Mom said, "Do me a favor and call your brother."

I told her I would, hung up and started crying uncontrollably. I felt like someone ripped my heart out and stomped on it. I called my brother, but I could hardly speak with him. I told him to call Mom and hung up. I cried all through the night until I finally passed out.

The next morning, my mother called to make sure I was all right. I said, "Yes, but I just can't think straight, and I feel like I want to die."

She told me to go find a priest to speak with. I told her I would and hung up the phone.

I found a priest, who I talked to for about an hour, which helped. I stopped at the store for something, and as I was walking in, I saw Patty and her new boyfriend drive by. She was sitting close to him, laughing. I felt like I was going to be sick again.

Every night at work for an entire week, I saw them act like newlyweds on our breaks.

At the end of our job, I said to Patty, "I'm leaving as soon as I get everything loaded in the car." I added, "If you're not here, you can walk home."

I quit smoking and drinking in 1979, and this experience almost pulled me back into it. But I had given all my pain, anger, and suffering to God throughout that week, spending countless hours praying desperately for His help. My prayers were answered, and He helped me find the courage and strength to resist the temptations and to get through this horrible time in my life.

All the way home, not a word was said. We lived in the same house, but in separate rooms. For the next two months, I had to work with her to fulfill our contracts because I couldn't go without work.

I was lying in bed at one of the casinos we were working at, when I woke up with chest pains. I called Patty's room, told her, and she said, "I'll be right there." A couple of minutes later, she was standing at my door.

She said, "Okay, what's wrong?"

I said, "I think I'm having a heart attack. I'm having pain in the left side of my chest and down my left arm."

She just laughed at me and said, "You need to grow up," turned, and walked away.

I lay there for a while until the pain stopped. I got up and went across the street to the casino where we were working. I sat at the bar, thinking about having a drink. A young security officer lady walked up to me and said, "Are you okay?"

I said, "I really don't know." She asked me what the problem was. I replied, "It's a long story." She told me she was a good listener.

She offered, "I get off in about ten minutes if you would like to talk."

When she returned, we talked for about two hours until I had to get ready for work. I felt so much better after our conversation. God sent me another angel to intervene because again, I did not give into temptation. I never saw the security guard again, and that casino was not a large casino. The guard simply disappeared.

After all our contracts were completed, I went my way and Patty went hers.

A few months later, Patty called me, wanting to borrow money to pay her rent. Shaking my head in disbelief,

I told her, "You have got to be kidding me! After what you did, you want me to pay your rent? Unbelievable!"

Before we split up, I'd co-signed for a brand-new car for her. Within four months, it was repossessed, and she wanted me to pay to could get it back.

Calmly I replied, "No, Patty, I can't help you. You did this to yourself. But you can tell your new boyfriend you need some help and see if he can help you out."

I thought that would be the last time I'd ever hear from Patty, but I was wrong. Soon she started calling me again like nothing had ever happened.

Chapter 47

Marty Robbins Tribute Shows Begin

I was working at a casino in Wendover, Nevada, when I met Jamie from Jamie's Rock 'n Roll Legends. On a night off, I went to another casino to watch a Legends show. The performer was walking around the tables, asking people to help him sing a Marty Robbins' song "Don't Worry About Me." He walked over to me, stuck the microphone in my face, and I started singing. I immediately got a standing ovation while I was singing, and the entertainer sat down in my chair, listening to me while I finished singing his song!

After the show, Jamie came out and introduced himself to me. He invited me to sing another song for him. I asked if he had a guitar I could use, so his lead player handed me his. As I sang El Paso, Jamie's mouth was wide open throughout the entire song.

He asked, "Are you working anywhere?"

I said, "Yes, at a casino down the street. I start at 3:00 p.m. tomorrow."

The next day at work, I found Jamie and his whole crew sitting in the front row. On my first break, I went down and spoke with him. Jamie asked, "Would you work for me as a Marty Robbin tribute artist?"

I had already been thinking about it through the night, so I replied, "Sure."

Jamie booked me all over the country performing Marty Robbins tributes. The shows were sold out everywhere we went. Our troupe consisted of Elvis Pressley, Dolly Parton, Kenny Rogers, and Marty Robbins tribute artists.

I went back to Sacramento to find someone to sing with me. That's where I met my third wife.

We decided to move to Las Vegas after I finished my contracts in Wendover. I booked myself into Bourbon Street, right off the main street in town.

A friend, who was a Tom Jones tribute artist, called to tell me there was a contest at Sunset Station, and that I should go and try out for it.

My friend and I went over and got our spots. The big night finally came for those who made it through, and soon contestants were eliminated one at a time. At the end of the night, there were four of us left: tribute artists Elvis from England, Sonny James from LA, a country star whose name I can't remember, and myself tributing Marty Robbins. The place was packed that night, and we were all extremely nervous. At the end of the show, when it was time to name The Tribute Artist of the Year, the announcer said, "Wait for it, wait for it, and the winner is: Marty Robbins, Mr. Roger Wade!"

I stood there, stunned. I found out all six judges voted for me! I couldn't believe I had finally won something in my life.

Afterward, I met a lady who told me she owned a talent agency. She gave me her business card and asked me to call her.

The next day when I called, she asked me to come down to her office. When I arrived, she greeted me and introduced me to a man leaving her office who looked just like Robin Williams. He shook my hand and walked out the door. She smiled at me and told me to sit down. She had pictures of "The Little Rascals" on the wall in her office. I told her they were my favorite entertainers. She said, "I was one of those kids" and pointed to Darla.

"Darla?" I asked and she nodded her head.

I thought that was so cool. From that day on, I became her number 1 entertainer. She had me performing all over Vegas. She bought me seven-hundred-dollar suits and took me to expensive dinners at some of the ritziest places in town.

Unfortunately, things didn't work out because I wouldn't sign an exclusive contract. I went my own way again.

I went to work in a club outside of Las Vegas, not knowing it would change my life forever.

Marty Robbins Tribute Shows

Chapter 48

Another Mysterious Encounter

After work while packing up my equipment, I noticed a couple in the corner of the bar. The bartender asked me to let them know it was closing time and they had to leave. When I got to their table, I gave them the bartender's message.

As the man slid out of the booth, he stumbled and fell on the floor—in my opinion, he was inebriated. I asked the lady if she could drive home or if she wanted me to call a cab. She said, "No need. I'll drive."

I finished loading my equipment, and I noticed two people arguing in a white pickup parked out in the parking lot. I didn't want to get involved in that drama, for sure. I had a long drive ahead, so I got in my car and drove away.

The road back to Vegas had a lot of dips and hills, so I drove with caution. I noticed a vehicle in my rear-view mirror that was quickly coming upon me. As it flew past me, I realized it was the same white truck I'd seen parked in the parking lot of the bar. As it went by, I saw the woman I'd spoken to in the bar sitting in the passenger's seat. That meant only one thing—the man I thought was inebriated was behind the wheel. Immediately I had a feeling this was not going to turn out well. I had a premonition of the vehicle overturned up ahead of me. I saw it in my mind.

As I came up over a hill, I noticed headlights beaming up through the dust on the side of the road. The pickup had overturned and rolled off the road.

I immediately pulled off the road, parked, grabbed my flashlight, and headed toward the white pickup. As I approached the vehicle, I could hear someone crying off to my right. It was the woman from the bar. She had been thrown from the vehicle to the side of the road. I ran up to her and asked, "Are you all right?"

She faintly replied, "Yes, I think so."

I told her to stay still and I would call for an ambulance. Even though I knew she wasn't alone, I asked her if she was alone anyway. I wanted to see if she was cognizant of her surroundings.

She stated her partner was in the truck and could I go check on him. I walked over to the truck to look for him. As I came around the side of the truck, a man approached me from the front of the truck. At the time, I paid no attention to where this man mysteriously came from because I was so focused on finding the man driving the truck. He walked beside me as I looked for the driver. I saw the driver about 8 feet from the truck, laying on his back. It was pitch-black, and we were in the middle of nowhere. There were no city lights to illuminate the sky. I didn't see his head at first and imagined that he might be decapitated. I told the man walking next to me what I thought.

He said, "No, he's not decapitated. His head is there." I went to the driver of the truck to check for a pulse. As I bent over him, he let out a sigh and then was quiet. I checked for a pulse, but there wasn't one. I knew he had passed.

Everything happened so fast that I hadn't even realized the man that had walked with me had disappeared. In fact, I didn't even know where he came from, for we were out in a desolate area, and there were no vehicles around except for the white truck and my car.

A car approached from the distance, and I flagged it down. I asked the driver the name of the road we were on because I wanted to call the police, but I didn't know where I was. I called the police and told them to report the accident. I stayed there with the woman until they arrived.

Everything was surreal. When the police questioned me, I didn't tell them about the man that walked to up to me that subsequently disappeared. (How do you explain to someone that there was someone there that wasn't there?)

A few days later, I saw an obituary in the local paper. The man in the picture was the man that I had walked with and talked with while searching for the driver of the white truck. He was the same man as the driver of the white truck. It is amazing that I didn't start drinking again after that experience.

Chapter 49

Bounty Hunting

Because I always wanted to be a bounty hunter, I found a place hiring and went to work for them. My first job was to find and pick up a bail jumper. I can't mention his name, so I'll just call him Jim. I had a great partner named Robert. We found out where Jim was hiding so we staked out the place. Jim's rap sheet read five feet, eight inches, 180 pounds, with brown hair. He was on his third count, so he was going back to prison.

I called for a couple more bounty hunters to back us up. As soon as they arrived, I told Robert and one of the others to watch the back door in case Jim decided to run.

I approached the front door and knocked. It was one of those doors with little glass diamond panes you could see through. A man came and opened the door, and when I looked up at him, he looked like the picture we had. However, this guy was close to six and a half feet tall and weighed about three hundred pounds. I called him by his name, he looked down at me, saw my badge and slammed the door. I took a step back, kicked the door open, and shattered those little diamond panes. I caught Jim just as he got to the kitchen and tackled him. While I was on top of him, hollering for Robert to come through the back door, another man came running down the hallway with a bat in his hand. I pulled my weapon and told him to stop, drop the bat, and hit the floor. When Robert came in, I had everything under control.

The funny part was how we had to put Jim in Roberts's car to take him to the police department. Robert drove a BMW with a sunroof. Jim was so large I had to put him in the front seat after I laid the seat all the way down. Then we had to put his left hand through the sunroof and the other out the window to handcuff them together. That's the way we road all the way to the station. On the way, I asked Robert if he wanted to stop for a bite. He just looked at me and laughed.

We made a great team. One day while we were riding around, we got a phone call from the guy we worked for. He told Robert he was firing him. When I asked why, he told me he only wanted white people working in his company. I told him he was a racist pig. I said, "You must not want me either. You fire Robert, you fire me."

He just said, "If that's the way you want it."

I think I called him every name I could think of before he hung up on me. I was so angry!

I moved to Monterey, California, and then Portland, Oregon. I still had contracts to fill so I had to find someone to help me. I had an extremely difficult time finding someone to perform with me as a duo. Whoever I hired didn't know enough material or didn't have a good work ethic. Either way, I eventually found someone to perform with me and everything was great after that.

Chapter 50

Arizona, Here We Come

My wife was a traveling nurse, and when her assignment was completed, we moved to Portland, Oregon. I went back to work repossessing vehicles and driving a tow truck. I even did some paranormal investigation! I soon realized that I was depressed about not performing. I told her that I wanted to move to Arizona. "What's in Arizona?" she asked.

"That's where Marty Robbins is from. Maybe I can perform there doing Marty Robbins tribute shows," I replied.

I purchased a motorhome from a friend, and we were off to Arizona—or so I thought. We got as far as Eugene, Oregon when the trouble with the motorhome began.

First, a belt broke, then the alternator went out. After they were repaired, the fuel pump went out. When we were finally back on the road, I wondered what else was going to happen with this motorhome.

We almost made it to Phoenix when the tire on the trailer pulling my motorcycle blew out. There we were, in the middle of the night, in the middle of nowhere, in the Arizona desert, with a flat tire. At least we had a place to sleep in the motorhome, so we were grateful for that.

When we awoke, we ventured outside. In the light of day, we found there was a small town within walking distance from us. When I say small, I mean a gas station and a restaurant. Another blessing, regardless. When I went to take the flat tire off the trailer, I realized I had no jack. I walked into town and went into the restaurant since the gas station was closed. I asked if anyone had a jack I could borrow. That's when I found out people in Arizona don't seem to have flat tires because no one had a jack in their car or truck. A nice waitress said she'd call the owner of the gas station to come and help me. Another blessing!

After forty-five minutes went by, we were on the road to Scottsdale. We pulled in around 1:30 a.m. I found a Walmart, where we stopped for the night. The next day we were on the 101 South when I saw a sign for a casino. We decided to park there for a while until we could find work. We called around and my wife got a nursing job that day. I pulled my bike from the trailer so I could take her to and from work. We saw an RV resort down the street from the casino and rented a space there for our motorhome.

On Halloween in our RV park, they were having a party at the gazebo. We decided to dress up and join everyone. We were listening to a lady play the keyboard. I asked her if I could sing a song and she said, "Why not?" I started singing and soon got everyone's attention. That night began my regular shows at our RV park. I also landed another regular gig, performing every Thursday night at a busy restaurant in Apache Junction, Arizona. With my wife working on-call nursing jobs all over town, and me performing at regular venues, we started bringing in good income.

Soon, we were able to buy a trailer in our park and gave away our motorhome to someone who needed a place to live. I always try my best to pay it forward.

One day, I was listening to a band perform at an RV sales center, which is where I met one of my best friends, Richard. He was the drummer for the band and had a great voice. We fast became brothers in a sense. In addition to performing, he was a truck driver, along with his lovely wife, Robin. They both quickly became family to me. There's nothing we wouldn't do for each other, and that still applies today. Occasionally, when they come out to see me perform, he sings with me as well.

Things were going well until my wife's alcohol addiction showed up. It had been well hidden in our marriage until she started coming home later and later from work, giving me all sorts of excuses for being late. One night I said to her, "I smell alcohol on your breath. You told me you didn't drink when we met. How long has this been going on?"

She blankly stared at me, having nothing to say other than "It was just one drink."

Over the following weeks, I realized she had a real addiction to alcohol. I tried to support her to quit, but she didn't think she had a problem. Realizing the problem was not going to be resolved, I decided that I might have to end my marriage. It was heartbreaking to me, but you can't make someone do what they don't want to do. Period. I had been through enough unhealthy relationships in my life not to see this blazing red flag.

I spent that afternoon, after making my decision, contemplating what was truly important to me. It was the only way I was ever going to find a partner to truly create a fulfilling life with.

The first thing I needed was a spiritual connection with someone. God is number 1 in my life. Next, I really wanted someone I could share music with—someone to sing with, who loved music and performing as much as I did. Of course, the next is a given: they had to be addiction free! I also wanted someone around me that I could be myself with and talk with about anything—someone who liked me as I am. Don't get me wrong—I have never said or thought I was perfect. I've had my share of demons to conquer. Now I was ready for someone to come into my life who truly cared for me, and we'd go forward from there. I prayed to God and asked for His guidance and help. The next night, my prayers were answered.

Chapter 51

God's Gracious Gift, Jeanne

I decided to spend the evening in search of a singing partner. It was around 9:00 p.m., and I was getting tired of clubs. I decided to try one more place in Scottsdale, a restaurant where they had nightly karaoke. I pulled my motorcycle into a parking space down the street from the restaurant. I wanted to walk a bit to do some thinking, so I didn't park to close. I walked in and sat down at a tall table against the wall, next to the dance floor. I started looking around the room to see if I knew anyone. I ordered a non-alcoholic beer and sat back to listen to the singers.

The next singer walked over to the dance floor, right in front of me, and started singing her song. She was casually dressed, and attractive. She had shoulder length blonde hair. She stood five feet, ten inches tall, which was about as tall as I am.

As I listened to her sing, I said to myself, "What a beautiful voice she has."

I wanted to talk to her, but she looked like the type of lady that was out of my class. I didn't have much confidence in myself at that time. My nerves stopped me from saying anything. I have always been the type of person that couldn't handle rejection, so I just sat back and listened.

After she finished singing, she went back to her table. Later she got up and walked toward me. My heart started pounding a little harder. Finally, she was standing at my table. She looked at me and said, "I'm Jeanne. We're all friends here. I wanted to invite you to join us in singing a song or two if you'd like."

I told her, "You don't want to hear me sing."

She replied, "Okay. Just thought I'd invite you to sing with us," as she turned and walked back to her table of friends.

I said to myself, "You just blew your chance to talk to her. You couldn't get any words out but that?"

I saw her say something to her girlfriend and they left through one of the side doors to the patio. I thought she'd left. What I didn't know at the time was that her friend was upset, and Jeanne went outside for a few minutes to privately do some healing (which is something else that Jeanne does to help people).

I decided to sing a song, "El Paso" by Marty Robbins. When I finished singing, I felt a tap to the back of my head. I turned around there she was, standing right behind me. I looked at her and she said, laughing, "You are such a liar. You have an amazing voice!"

She asked if she could sit down. I said, "Thank you," as I motioned for her join me.

She pulled up a chair and started talking to me, but I couldn't hear what she was saying because the music was so loud. I apologized to her, telling her I couldn't hear what she was saying. I asked if she would like to go out on the patio and talk. She agreed, so we walked outside to a table where it was quiet. After some casual conversation, I asked her if she'd like to take a walk. She said, "That would be nice. We can walk down to the park—it's a few blocks away."

We walked for what seemed like a lifetime, but it was only a few hours. I explained that I was going through a rough time with my marriage, and I had already decided to file for a divorce. I told her, "Things are not working out, with no hope of getting better, and I've had enough." I was trying to be as honest as I could be.

We spoke about music, both hers and mine, and we agreed to exchange our CDs that next day. She gave me her number, and I told her I would call her that next day.

It was getting late, so I walked with her to her truck. She asked me where I had parked, and I pointed to my motorcycle. It was right beside her truck! Of all the parking spaces in downtown Scottsdale, we were parked next to each other! We looked at each other with open mouths and started laughing, and then we went our separate ways.

The next day, I called Jeanne, got directions to her apartment, and brought her my CD. She invited me in, and we spent a few more hours talking. Jeanne told me about Reiki and donating sessions at a local domestic violence shelter for the past five years. She told me how she had earned her first, second, and master teacher and practitioner degrees over the past ten years. I had never heard of Reiki before. She offered me a free session. She said, "You are going through so many changes and overwhelming emotions right now. A session may help bring some peace and clarity," and I agreed.

After the session, I felt different somehow—more alive more relaxed. Jeanne also owned a window cleaning business. It was getting late, so I told her I had to go,—though I really didn't want to. I knew she worked very early in the morning to stay out of the intense afternoon Arizona heat. There was something about her that was so different from any other person I'd ever met. I had a lot to think about on that ride back the trailer.

Jeanne M. Danowski, Reiki master
She is a very wise and compassionate woman.

Chapter 52

Attention Deficit Disorder

We became great friends, and Jeanne taught me a lot about myself. She suspected that I had attention deficit disorder. She told me with a laugh, "My first clue was how you told me you drink strong coffee all day up until bedtime and sleep soundly!"

I had no idea what she was talking about. We sat down, and she explained to me that caffeine is calming to people who have ADD. I told her, "I've probably had it all my life!"

Later she and my mom encouraged me to seek professional help for they both realized I was deeply depressed. Seeking help was one of the best decisions I ever made. Not only did I suffer from ADD, but I found out I suffered from PTSD as well.

Those realizations opened a whole new world for me. I had probably been depressed but learned to cope and survive throughout my entire childhood. I also realized I wasn't just another dumb kid, and all the things that had happened to me growing up was connected to ADD. I wondered what my life would have been like if I hadn't had ADD. Finally, I understood why it seemed impossible to concentrate and why I was unable to read a book all the way through. I thought about what it would be like to sit and think without my mind wandering continuously. My early years had been so frustrating. The only two things I could do were perform and martial arts. Every other type of job I had, I ended up losing because I would get bored with it—not enough excitement for me. I always had to keep moving, keep busy, keep active. Music is the only career I've ever enjoyed. It keeps me on my toes, and it is always different, always exciting.

Jeanne seemed interested in my life and what I had accomplished. I've always had friends that wanted to be around me just because I was playing music and they wanted to be in the limelight, as they say. Thanks to her, I have a lot of people around me who are true friends now, and I know the difference. She's the first person, other than my mother, who wanted to hear about my life, and not spend time talking about herself. It was really a great day.

Jeanne is amazing; she has done so much to help me get my life back on track, and she's taught me a lot about life in general. I would have to write another book just to describe everything!

While I was waiting for my divorce to be finalized, I realized I couldn't stay in the trailer. When I told her I had nowhere to go and didn't know what I was going to do, Jeanne offered me her second bedroom until I could get my bearings and back on my feet. My whole life changed the minute I stepped through her door.

We started going out as friends, having a lot of fun just being together. We began singing together as well. Jeanne kept her window cleaning business. We'd wash windows by day and perform by night!

We also spent time with my soon to be ex-wife, who told me Jeanne and I were meant to be together. She told me she was happier being single, but that didn't last long. She became engaged that same year and moved up to the White Mountains to live with her new fiancé.

When Jeanne and I realized we had fallen in love, we officially became a couple, and a very happy one at that.

Chapter 53

A Gift of a Lifetime

Out of the blue one day, Jeanne asked me if we could go to a motorcycle dealership in Scottsdale and just look around. She knew I loved to ride my bike, but my bike had seen better days. I was unable to ride it because of the repairs it needed and the fact that it was unsafe to ride. When we arrived at the dealership, she told me to look around. She asked me, "What motorcycle would you get if you could have any one you want? Go find it."

I told her, "I'd love to have any Harley," as we began to walk around the dealership.

I took her to the one I liked the best, and I said, "If I bought that one, I'd want it to be red and black."

Jeanne said she had to do something and that she would be right back. I was sitting on the same bike when she walked up to me. She asked, "Are you sure that's the one you want?"

I started laughing and said, "Yes, I'll take it home with me today."

She looked at me and said, "I'm sorry, but you'll have to wait to take it home. They don't have that color in stock and have to make it for you. It might be a month or so before you can get it."

I looked at her and said, "Oh, okay," and started laughing.

The next thing I knew, a saleswoman walked up to me with a beautiful red helmet and a T-shirt in her hands. She presented them to me and congratulated me on my new motorcycle.

I just looked at Jeanne and said, "Okay, this isn't funny anymore."

Jeanne smiled and said, "This isn't a joke. Your new bike should arrive in a month or so.

I just about passed out. The cost of that motorcycle was $25,000! No one, other than my mother, has ever done anything like that for me before. I was at a total loss for words. All I could get out of my mouth was a simply thank you. She told me, "You are so worth it! Enjoy!"

After we returned from working out of town for a few weeks, my bike was ready to pick up. It was raining lightly, but it wasn't rain I was wiping from my eyes. I smiled and cried all the way home. I was the happiest guy in the world.

But Jeanne is always like that. She loves to bring joy to others, and she loves to see and bring goodness in the world. She is a lot like me in that way. So began our quest to bring joy and goodness to the world together.

My 2007 Harley Davidson Electro Glide Classic

Jeanne and I Christmas in Utah

Chapter 54

Our New Life in the White Mountains

One day, my ex-wife and her fiancé called me and asked if I wanted the trailer as a present. They told me they wanted to get married as soon as the divorce was final. I said yes and thanked them.

I told Dawn how glad I was that they had found each other. Around this time Jeanne was having serious problems tolerating the heat in the summer, so Dawn and her fiancé offered us their spare bedroom for the summer until we could find a place of our own. Another blessing.

We got along with them well. They helped us get a job playing music down the road from where they lived. I agreed to do work for him outside the house and Jeanne took care of the inside of the house and cooked in exchange for rent. It worked out well.

I rebuilt his shed, kept his lawn looking good, repaired his driveway, and put in a new walkway to the house. Jeanne and I were also washing windows on our time off and I went to work for a rancher rounding up cattle and mending and building fences.

That lasted through the summer, and then we went back down to the valley and started playing music through the season, which lasted until April. We still washed windows on our days off. This became our normal—performing in summer in the White Mountains, staying with friends, and performing in winter in the Valley, living in our trailer. We still washed windows on our days off. We were busy. We were grateful. We were blessed.

Our little beach house

Home sweet home

Chapter 55

Midnight Moon Duo

The story with Jeanne and me keeps getting better and better. We've been fortunate to become one of the most popular duos in the Valley. I've enjoyed performing Marty Robbins Tribute Shows, from Estes Park in Colorado to Music Ranch Montana in Montana, all over the Valley and in the White Mountains.

While pursuing work in the White Mountains, we decided to stop in a local RV park and drop off our CD. That's where we met Arlene "Strannie" Strandberg. Jeanne went in, spoke with her, gave her a CD, and thanked her for her time. We later received a call from Strannie, asking us to play for a dance, and we have been playing there ever since. The funny part to this story is Strannie took the CD home to play for her roommate Ruth. Ruth exclaimed, "That's my window washer, Jeanne!"

What are the odds? Jeanne has washed windows for Ruth in the valley for over twenty years and never met Strannie and never knew they lived together.

Over the past seventeen years, we have had many of those experiences—synchronicity at its best! It proves to me that we are always in the right place at the right time when we follow our intuition and have faith. We would stress over getting enough jobs in the past and soon learned that God always provides for us—every time. When we lose a gig, two or three come in to replace it shortly after losing it—and they are always better than the one we lost. We both agree, we go where God directs us to go, to where we are meant to be, to do what we are meant to do. We always find out why later, and they are always great stories!

Chapter 56

The Good Stuff

We performed in Show Low for the summer and then headed back to the valley in the fall to perform there. One thing is for certain—when we need work, God always blesses us with it. A few weeks out of each year, we went see my mother. We sometimes performed for the residents of the apartment complex she lived in. It helped with our expenses, but more importantly, we were able to bring some music, fun, and joy to the residents. I loved seeing my mom beam with pride when we did perform there. She's always been my biggest fan and supporter, and I love making her proud of me.

As time went on, Jeanne and I became one of the most popular duos around the valley. The more places we played, the more jobs we got. I wish I could name all the people who have support us and followed us to our dances. All I can say is I have more friends than I could ever imagine I would have had in my lifetime. From coast to coast and all throughout Canada, the list goes on and on. We have become extended members of many families over the years, enjoying life just doing what God intended us both to do. There is a deep satisfaction performing, but it is the love and thousands of friendships over the past seventeen years that fulfill us the most. Thanks to all of you for your love and support. I love and appreciate every one of you.

Along the way, we met Dale and Bev Owens at one of our shows. Dale is Buck Owens' cousin. It's funny because I'm from the Bakersfield area and know Dales's other cousins. I've worked with most of them throughout my career.

The Owens had retired from their own gospel group called "The Joy Gospel Singers." When the four of us started performing gospel shows together, they were a big hit. These two are great performers who made our shows even better. God brings us right to where we need to be, doing exactly what we need to do. Performing together gave us an opportunity to praise the Lord again and enjoy a deeper fellowship with all our friends as well.

We did some shows at the mining camp restaurant in Apache Junction for many years before it sadly burnt down. Our first show there was a country tribute show, the second was a Gospel show. The biggest show was my Marty Robbins tribute show, which sold out just about every night. The following year we performed a full week of Marty Robbins tribute shows—three shows a day, seven days a week!

We continued to perform at many local RV Resorts, mostly happy hours and dances. We also found work doing private parties, performing at great restaurants and even began to get ballroom dance gigs. Those ballroom dances gave us an opportunity to perfect our tempos, making it much more enjoyable for the dancers.

At all those venues, every time, something happened that was extraordinarily healing for someone. We were always in the right place at the right time for the right reason. We brought joy and enjoyed an immense fellowship with the Lord and all those around us. This is "the good stuff" we've enjoyed and will enjoy for many years to come—simply answering God's call to go where He takes us, to be with whom we are meant to be with.

We regularly experienced deeply rewarding moments when we performed at retirement homes. Many of the residents didn't get out in the world, so it was fun to bring the world of music and memories to them. I will always remember the day a woman came up to me in tears, smiling at me. She said, "That song was our wedding dance. Bless you for bringing back that wonderful memory." She told us about losing her husband a few years back. We played that song for her every time we saw her.

We performed songs from the forties to the eighties, so we always found favorite songs for everyone. That became our trademark and the cornerstone of what we do in our performances—taking people back in time to relive wonderful memories. Seeing the joy and smiles on so many faces means the world to us, and why we go through what we go through to be able to perform. It is not an easy life, but it is extremely rewarding.

Jeanne and Roger (Midnight Moon Duo)

Chapter 57

Angels Working Overtime

One day, while Jeanne and I were talking about my health, she asked me if I ever had a colonoscopy—to which I replied, "No."

She asked me if she could make me an appointment to have one done, adding she had a strong feeling it should be sooner rather than later. One thing I've learned is to trust Jeanne's intuition. Most of the time it surprises me how she comes up with things from out of the blue, but I always trust her intuition now. I had it done as soon as they could get me in. They found five precancerous polyps. They were all removed, but one. It was too large to remove that day, so I had to come back to remove it. When they finally removed it, they found it was benign, but there was a sixth polyp hiding behind the big one that was also pre-cancerous. I went back 1 year later, and all was clear. I now go back every five years and so far, so good—all clear. Thank you, God, and thank you, God, for Jeanne. Thank you, Jeanne!

We've had some challenges playing music. It's not an easy life and there have been some major disappointments. Many people don't realize what a cutthroat business this can be. It can also take a toll on your health and well-being.

Some of our challenges have included commitments being broken—even though we had a signed contract—without warning, we've had to sue to get payment; we've been cancelled and had entire summers ruined—putting us into financial struggle; we've had to deal with bad checks, nonpayment, and late payments; we've been "gossiped" about and even sabotaged.

We have poured our hearts, souls, and time into doing the best performances we can for everyone, every show. We've made sacrifices and many times struggled to perform everywhere we have. No, it is not an easy road to travel. I've learned to control my temper, watch my anger, and do a lot of deep breathing over the years. I wish I'd learned to do this sooner. I found out I'd had a heart attack in my forties from the scar tissue damage they found during my surgery, which is the next story I want to share with you.

After we got back from our Colorado road trip, I had to go in for my checkup at our cardiologist. They wanted us to come in twice a year for checkups, so that's what we did. Jeanne passed hers, but I did not. They had me do a stress test. I didn't pass that. They had me do a nuclear stress test and I didn't pass it either. The ultrasound confirmed that they needed me to get an angiogram. Okay, I'm telling myself, "This is not good."

Jeanne had another one of her "strong feelings" to make the appointment at the hospital in Scottsdale North, rather than the hospital at Osborn. Again, I trusted her intuition. While I was still under after the angiogram was completed, the doctor came out and told Jeanne that I had what is called a Widow Maker. He told her I had three blocked arteries and surgery needed to be performed ASAP.

He told Jeanne we could go home and call to schedule it for that week. Jeanne told the doctor she didn't feel right taking me home, knowing this shocking information and knowing my life was in jeopardy. She asked if I could be admitted, and the surgery done right then and there at the hospital. By now, I was awake and alert and educated as to what was happening. The doctor asked if that's what I wanted to do, and I said, "Absolutely. Let's get it done."

The doctor said, "Fine. Let's schedule it for tomorrow," and he did just that.

They checked me into the hospital, got me a room and we waited for the surgeon to come speak with us. I didn't know I even had heart disease, much less a heart attack.

Chapter 58

Triple Bypass

As I lay in my hospital bed, I tried to recall any incidents where I may have had warnings of heart disease. I remembered something that happened in Las Vegas. I was heading to go to my martial arts class when I started, I felt sharp needle-like pain in the left side of my chest as I started to get in my truck. I felt clammy, so I sat down on the ground next to the truck. In a little while I felt better, so I got up and drove to class.

That night in class, we were running and tumbling over three people on their hands and knees. When I did my jump, I hit the mat on my right shoulder and dislocated it. My sensei asked me if I was okay, and I asked him to look at my shoulder. He suggested I go to the hospital. I asked him to help me put my shoulder back in place as I stood next to one of the walls. I put my back to the wall as he hit me sharply on the front of my shoulder. Pop goes the weasel! Back in place it went. I put on a scarf one of the girls had around my neck and arm and went on with class. After class, I went to the hospital like I promised, and the doctor put a sling on my arm. The next day I was back in class, but

I could only use my left arm. One week later, I was back to my old self, feeling fine.

Back to the present moment. I realized we were thinking the same thoughts when Jeanne said, "Let's not go home and stress about this, thinking and waiting—let's get it done now while you are here and safe."

They checked me in and Jeanne stayed with me until I was released a week later. She would not leave my side. The night before surgery we were watching a funny television show, laughing, and keeping a positive attitude. Abruptly a doctor came in the room, glaring at us both, exclaiming, "I guess you don't realize how serious this is! You have what is called a widow maker."

The doctor changed the channel to a blank screen and pulled up my angiogram! Her demeanor was serious and harsh. Jeanne immediately said, "We know exactly what Roger has, what needs to be done and how serious this is. What we don't need is to be reminded of it—we're trying to chill out and relax tonight and think about anything else. Please leave—freaking out and being afraid is the last thing he or I need right now." As she left the room, we looked at each other with the same thought—did that just happen?

We turned the channel back to our program and thankfully started to relax again, holding hands. The staff had brought in a recliner for Jeanne so she could sleep next to me. Jeanne had a feeling we were not alone. It was so peaceful and calm in our room. She decided to take some photos around the room with her phone. When we saw the pictures, they were filled with orbs—they were all around us! We prayed silently together before we fell asleep. Part of my prayer was thanking God for my incredible life and if it was His will to take me, I was ready. I truly didn't think I would survive the surgery and was prepared to leave this world that night. I was surprisingly peaceful. I looked at Jeanne and told her how much I appreciated her in my life and how deeply I loved her. She said the same to me, we kissed, hugged, and slept soundly through the night.

My doctor came in bright and early next morning. He said, "Are you ready to go? Let's get this done!" He was young, upbeat, and experienced and made us both feel confident. Yes, I was ready to go.

Next, staff came in and took me to the pre-surgical area where they shaved me, and not my face either.

I remember a real pretty nurse came in with a razor in her hand and said, "We are going to have to shave you." Then she turned and walked out of the room and in walked a big woman speaking with a Russian-sounding accent. She said, "I'm going to shave you now!" Yikes!

Someone came in and started an IV. The next thing I know, I was being wheeled down a long hallway. Jeanne told me later that I was singing "El Paso" all the way to surgery. The day before I was telling my doctor about my Marty Robbins show last week and had given him a CD to listen to.

After the surgery was over, Jeanne told me that she'd asked my doctor if he played music during the surgery.

He said, "Yes, but it wasn't country!"

When it was all over, I was lying in ICU with Jeanne right there beside me, waiting for me to wake up. When I opened my eyes, it was like seeing an angel standing next to my bed. I don't remember too much about what went on that day so here's what Jeanne told me.

I had a huge oxygen mask over my face, which was making me extremely stressed. She got the nurse, and they decided to put something smaller on me, which was so much better. The nurses in ICU were very concerned that I was not speaking yet. Jeanne asked that they give her a tablet for me to write on. They told her that they wanted me to speak, not write.

Jeanne said, "Trust me. Give me something for him to write on," which they did.

I took the chalk and scribbled on the little chalkboard "teeth." Everyone laughed as the nurse got my dentures, put them in, and I shot everyone a big grin! Then I started talking—a lot!

The next story Jeanne told me was about my first attempt out of bed, going for a walk around ICU. My nurses were young, pretty, and very sweet. They helped me up and provided a wheelchair to hold onto the back of while I attempted to walk. Jeanne said I was waving at everyone in each room, saying hello as I walked by. She told me that I even said, "Oh, you don't look so good. I hope you feel better" as I passed one room. Jeanne said she just shook her head and we proceeded on.

At one point, I waived to the head nurse at the end of the corridor, and she waived back. Her hand waive was slight, from side to side. Supposedly, I blurted out, "That is so cool. Where did you learn to do that?"

The head nurse replied, laughing, "You don't learn that. You earn it."

When I made my way around the ICU back to my room, my two nurses helped me back into bed. One of the nurses said, "You get his left leg, I'll get the other and we'll get him laid in bed."

Jeanne told me that I misunderstood what they said, and I replied to the two young nurses, "I really don't have it in me right now." She said everyone had a good laugh and a few blushes.

I do remember our dear friends Robin and Richard came in to see me. Robin sat on the edge of my bed and held my hand, angel number two. This is just one of a million reasons why I love these two so much.

Jeanne and I spent the rest of the week holding hands, hanging out and talking. Jeanne watched over me like an angel would, never leaving my side.

Here comes the drama. The day I was supposed to go home someone gave me an insulin shot I wasn't supposed to have. It almost threw me into a diabetic shock. Thank God Jeanne was there because she ran out and grabbed one of the nurses. The nurse literally flew in the door with a huge glass of orange juice and that set me right. The next day we got to go home.

For two months, I had to sleep in our recliner. You can't imagine what I couldn't do for myself. Jeanne had to help me take a shower, help me out of the chair and take care of me like she always does. I can tell you right now if it wasn't for her, I wouldn't have written this book because I wouldn't be here right now. She is the one who told me I need to go in for regular checkups. I wouldn't have even thought of it. The doctor told me I wouldn't have made it very much longer without having a massive heart attack that could have killed me. Thank you, Jeanne Danowski. Thank you, Jesus!

Chapter 59

Our Life Now

Almost seven months passed after that open-heart surgery, which changed my life forever, and everything got back to normal—if you call our lives normal! We've had many grand adventures, challenges, setbacks, and accomplishments.

I did have another heart attack when one of my stents failed. I also experienced pancreatitis due to taking my ADD medication over the years.

During this time, it was also discovered that I had numerous gallstones in my gallbladder. The doctors and I decided my gallbladder would be removed if the high pancreatic enzyme levels came down significantly. They doubted that they would come down in one day, though, to be able to perform the surgery the next morning. They left me to get some rest that night, saying they would recheck my levels in the morning. What happened that night was another miracle. Praise God!

Around 9:00 p.m., the pastor from a resort park we performed at and his wife came in to see us. When they entered the room, we visited for a bit. Suddenly the pastor's wife said, "Let's do what we came here to do—pray over Roger."

The pastor laid his hands over my pancreas. His wife laid her hands over the pastor's. Jeanne laid her hands over the pastor's wife's hands. I laid my hands on top of them all. The pastor spoke out loud his prayers for a total healing for me of all conditions and asked God to speed up the process if it could be sped up. You could feel the room get warm, and everyone got chills as we prayed together. When the prayers were finished, we all hugged, and we thanked them as they left for home.

Early the next morning, the nurse came in and drew my blood to check my enzyme levels. A while later, the doctor came in and said, "Are you ready to have that gallbladder removed?"

He informed us that not only had the enzyme levels come down, but they came down better than they needed them to be to perform the surgery. He also stated he had never seen anything like that before. We told him about what we did the night before, and he said, "It sure sounds like a miracle to me!"

The surgery was textbook and successful, and I was released the next day. I have never had a problem with any of that since.

After recuperating from my gallbladder surgery, we began performing again when another whammy happened—COVID. After we were exposed to COVID, our doctor immediately put us on the protocol President Trump used, including ivermectin. The protocol stopped the COVID in its tracks in a matter of days. We ended up in the hospital for a day from dehydration as we couldn't stop the diarrhea we were both battling. The hospital continued the protocol we were already on and got us both rehydrated. Unfortunately, Jeanne contracted community pneumonia in the hospital. Her liver and kidney function levels were skyrocketing. They gave her enough antibiotics for a football team, our doctor later told her. She told me afterward about her miracle in the hospital. She relayed to me the doctors kept coming in and out of her room, worried about these high levels. I started a prayer chain on social media on both our pages. We had hundreds upon hundreds of fans, friends, and family praying with us continuously. Jeanne stayed on her phone on her page to distract her. She told me on the third day when she got on her page, she immediately read a post from our friend, Vivienne, beseeching Jesus to intervene on her behalf and for Him to bring about a total, complete, and immediate healing. In that moment, Jeanne told me she got chills, and every hair on her body stood on end. A very short while later, they came in to draw her blood again to see if there was any improvement. They came back in an hour or so and said that unbelievably, her levels were normal and that they were taking her to rehab to recuperate since she couldn't get proper care at home. I could not take care of her as I was recuperating myself and very weak. She made a full recovery in two weeks and came home. Another incredible miracle. Thank You, Jesus. Thank you, Vivienne, and all the prayer warriors who diligently prayed continuously for both of us.

Both of us survived COVID, but we lost everything we built over fifteen years. The shutdown lasted over a year, deleting our shows one after the other. However, I can say that whatever we go through, God is always at the forefront and our faith is strong. We just take each day at a time, grateful for what we have been given, grateful for what we have and grateful for what is yet to be given us by God.

Through thick and thin, we've been blessed countless times. Our family and our fans, who've become our friends and extended families, have been with us every step of our way, as a host of earthly angels—helping us and supporting us financially, emotionally, and spiritually. The words "thank you" seem to fail when we speak them, for they could never convey the depth of our gratitude or the love we feel inside for so many. For those of you reading this book and know who you have been and are to us, and we thank you from our hearts to yours. We are blessed to have you in our lives.

Jeanne and countless friends and family encouraged me to write this book about my life. I did so in hopes of providing support to those making their way through life's challenges. Growing up with ADD held me back from doing a lot of things I wanted to do, but I just kept fighting it and I moved on with my life.

Life is a precious gift from God, and if you need help don't hesitate to ask for it. If you need someone to talk to, reach out and find someone or go talk to a clergyman. Just don't do what I did and hold everything in until you explode. Remember, the past is behind you, and the present is what matters. I have learned to live in this present moment, for that is all there really is.

Don't walk through life backward. You must take that step forward and keep walking. A wise person once told me, "If you want something bad enough in this life, you can get it. God will give it to you, but you must work for it and be open and willing to receive it."

I wasn't certain I would ever finish writing this book. Every time I got halfway through it, I'd go back and add something else. It was emotionally draining to relive in depth so many horrendous experiences and exhilarating to relive my grandest accomplishments and all the miracles. Together, Jeanne and I have a deep love for God and all humanity that fuels our deepest desires to help lift others wherever and whenever we can. This was truly a labor of love: self-love, for I was healed throughout the process of writing this book.

Did I make it to "the big time" as an entertainer? Yes, my dream of being a great entertainer came true, at least in my heart it did. Never give up on yourself and always remember you are responsible for what you do in this life. You gotta have faith (the title to one of my gospel songs) in God and in yourself and take one day at a time.

God bless you and may you fly on the wings of angels, all the days of your life.

Acknowledgments

First and foremost, I thank the Lord for the gifts and talents He's given to me, and his never-ending love, guidance, and support. My path is His path, always providing what I need to walk it. Each day, I look forward to the new adventures He'll take me on.

I thank my mother, Bulah Wade, for her constant love, support, and faith in me. She's the best Mom a guy could have—my friend, my confidant, and my biggest fan! She's been with me through thick and thin, ups and downs, and everything in between. I owe her a debt I could never repay, and I'm blessed she has been with me all my life.

Where do I start, thanking Jeanne Danowski? From the moment we met she believed in me—helped me feel special—and told me I deserved to feel special because I was special. She supports and encourages me to pursue my heart's desires and jumps in to help me in whatever way she can to "get the job done." She is the love of my life, my true soulmate, and a true partner in every sense of the word. I love you, Jeanne, and I am so grateful you walked over to me the night we met. I also want to extend appreciation to her family—Marjorie Danowski, Tom and Anne Danowski, Mary Anne Cleary, and my new angel watching over me, Dave Cleary. You make me feel welcome, loved, and supported!

Roger L Wade

Thank you to Arlene "Strannie" Strandberg for editing this book—the longest paragraph she ever read! I don't even know how you did it, but I am so grateful for all the time and attention you gave my book to bring it to life. Bless you.

I would like to give special thanks to Audrey and Al Zimmerman for believing in me and helping me get this book published. I couldn't have done it without you, dear friends.

To Richard and Robin McAtee, my extended family, thank you for being in my life. You are the reason I was able to begin performing in Arizona to start this journey. Your support, belief, and faith in me means the world to me.

A huge thanks goes out to our friends Debbie and Phil Robertson, Tammy Moore, Dawn and Jim, Tawny and Clay Russell, Keith and Mimi Huntley, Marvin and Louise Wiens, Frank and Kay Reed, Ruth Swanson and Arlene Strandberg, and Jerry and Marion Byrne for their extraordinary generosity providing Jeanne and I a place to live when we needed one. Thank you to Eva and Bruce Sutphen for storing our belongings while we were in transition, helping us through COVID, and your support and friendship. During the direst moments over the past ten years, special friends, particularly Maura and Dick McConnell and Candace and Brad Starr, stepped in to organize fundraisers to help keep us going. I am grateful to them and all who helped and supported us at those fundraisers. I couldn't have written this book without you.

I have been blessed to have so many friends, family and fans extending support to me over my entire life's journey. With your support I've been able to keep moving forward, including writing this book. Thank you for your friendship and support over the years.

The road to writing this book was strewn with many challenging moments, but I always had a huge support system through family, friends, and fans to make it through.

God bless you all and keep you all the days of your lives.

About the Author

Roger Wade was born in Bakersfield, California. He began playing rhythm guitar when he was six, which led to the discovery of his many musical talents. Roger has accompanied well-known recording artists such as Merle Haggard, Billy Mize, Billy Armstrong, Bonnie Owens, Joe and Rose Lee Maphis, Kay Austin, Dolly Parton, Trisha Yearwood, and Jean Shepard over the years. Struggling with undiagnosed attention deficit disorder for the first sixty years of his life, Roger found that the only two things that calmed him and helped with his focus were music and martial arts. He resides in the White Mountains of Arizona with his partner, Jeanne Danowski, where he enjoys performing, writing, and working with leather tooling.

Printed in the USA
CPSIA information can be obtained
at www.ICGtesting.com
JSHW020353280723
45465JS00002B/5

9 798887 512211